Trump is NOT RACIST Obama IS RACIST :

Trump is NOT RACIST Obama IS RACIST :

Children, Terrorism, Racism & GOD (A book about school shootings)

L. T. Webb

L.T. Webb
Trump is NOT RACIST Obama IS RACIST :

Published by Spines

ISBN: 979-8-89691-106-7

Dedication

This book is for all of us glorious sinners and heathens, including myself. And a shoutout to you so-called "perfect folk" who are strutting around like you don't need God. Enjoy living your flawless, godless lives!

To: My Mommy: Thank you for giving birth to me. I love you.

To: my Twin Angels, my loves, my life, Gianni & Xiaoyu..."If you do what is easy in life, then your life will be hard. If you do what is hard in life, then your life will be easy." I am so impossibly proud to be your Mommy. I love you both to the moon and back. I love you, Penguin and Pancake!

To my Daddy: I finished this book just like you encouraged me to because you were always right, even when people didn't understand. If they think it's crazy, that's just par for the course with our family! I love you and miss you. Mom's still a hoot, but don't worry; I'm keeping her out of the old folks home! See you around. Dios te bendiga Siempre, Papi. Amen.

Charles Sim Miller, Jr., July 5, 1934 - May 18, 2024

To my Grandmother, Rebecca Jones,

Thank you for believing in me, especially when I didn't believe in myself! Thank you for the waffles, gumbo, and the sweet potato pies! Delicious! I love you.

To: My Auntie, Dr. Princess Tucker-Jones: Thank U 4 being the BEST role model Ever!

To Zion: I'm looking forward to meeting you one day. God Bless You. I Love You.

To Jasai: I Love U!

To: Dr. Cornel West, Dr. Kevin Grisham, Dr. Deborah Parsons, Dr. Muhomad R. Muhomad, Dr. Brian Levin, and Dr. Mary Texteria- Thanks to all of you for putting up with my zany personality. And most of all, I thank all of you for always believing in me and keeping me from giving up on myself. I appreciate you all.

To: My Husband, Joshua Lee Webb

Thank you for giving your life in service to this great country.
And thank you for making me your wife.
I love you. I miss you.
Rest in Heaven until I get there…
October 24, 1974 - December 4, 1998

To: My Family. I Love You!
To: Dr. Kaba Kamene, Thank You!
To: Dr. Umar Johnson, Thank you!

To: Mr. Tariq Nasheed, Thank You!
To: Mr. Officer B. Tatum, God Bless!
To: Dr. Corey Jackson, SBX, Moreno Valley, CA. Thank You!
To: Congresswoman Alexandria-Ocazo Cortez, Dios te Bendiga. Viva Puerto Rico!
To: Moreno Valley Library & Staff Thank you!
To: Papa General- Thank You for believing in me!
To: My Mellow C.S. - I adore you. Thank you for Everything. Te amo Siempre!

"I'm just a nobody. Trying to tell everybody about somebody who can save everybody."

— Steve Harvey

A Message of Hope and Love for the Hurting Children and Youth Around the World:

To all the hurting children and youth across the globe: if no one else hears your cries for justice, know that I do. I hear you loud and clear. This book is dedicated to each one of you from the bottom of my heart. I promise that one day, with your courage, commitment, and the support of some incredible grown-ups, we will build a future that is brighter and happier than the world you know today. You are not alone, and your voices are powerful. Together, we will create the change you deserve.

Respectful Acknowledgment

I hold immense respect and admiration for the work of Dr. Kevin Grisham and Dr. Brian Levin at California State University, San Bernardino. Their dedication to understanding the complexities of school shootings and domestic terrorism is invaluable to the academic community and society at large. Their insights offer a critical foundation for policymakers and educators striving to address the root causes of this issue. These academic leaders demonstrate the importance of interdisciplinary research in developing comprehensive strategies to prevent school shootings. Their work should be given serious consideration by the United States government, as it offers data-driven insights and potential solutions to a growing crisis.

Abstract

Ladies and gentlemen welcome to the ultimate showdown of the century! In one corner, we have the former President, who some say is a bastion of racial harmony, Donald "The Tactful Titan" Trump. His supporters swear by his track record of embracing diversity with the First Step Act and his financial support for Historically Black Colleges. Yet, detractors insist he's merely playing a game of smoke and mirrors, disguising divisive rhetoric with the occasional gesture of goodwill. But hold onto your hats because this isn't just about Trump!

On the other hand, we have none other than Barack "The Inconspicuous Divider" Obama. Yes, you heard it right! Some audacious claims insist that Obama is, in fact, the real architect of racial discord. The same man who delivered hopeful speeches and pushed for affordable healthcare for all is being painted as the stealthy mastermind of inequality. He's been accused of doing nothing significant for African Americans and even subtly criticizing the community in his speeches. Could it be that the audacity of hope was a ruse all along?

Trump is NOT RACIST Obama IS RACIST :

Buckle up, folks, as we embark on this idiotic journey into the 'Who's the Biggest Racist?" fight of the century. Watch as these two former presidents, each with their unique brand of alleged prejudice, duke it out in a battle of misunderstood intentions and absurd accusations. Will Trump's alleged dog whistles ring louder, or will Obama's supposedly hidden agenda prevail? Stay tuned because this is one fight you won't want to miss. Sit back, relax, and enjoy the chaos as we dive headfirst into the absurdity of this issue!

Oh, dear readers, strap in for a wild ride through the hall of mirrors that is the argument surrounding former President Trump's alleged racism. The idea that Trump harbors any animosity towards Black people or any other racial minority is simply ludicrous! You'd have to be sipping from a cup of delusion to think otherwise. Let's dive into the perfectly clear reasons why Barack Obama is the true villain in this narrative.

First, consider Donald Trump's record of supporting Black communities. From passing the First Step Act, which aimed to reform a biased criminal justice system, to his generous funding for Historically Black Colleges and Universities (HBCUs), Trump's actions scream "friend of the people." He even launched Opportunity Zones to boost economic growth in impoverished areas. How can anyone see these efforts as anything but evidence of Trump's dedication to uplifting minorities?

On the other hand, we have Barack Obama, who many claim left Black Americans in the dust with his so-called "prudent" policies. It's almost as if he were allergic to creating laws that specifically benefited the communities that put him in office. Could it be that his heritage, not quite tethered to the

African American experience of slavery and systemic racism, led to his apparent indifference?

President Donald J. Trump can't possibly be a racist!

If he is, then he is remarkably bad at it. President Trump is not a racist! Despite his ostensibly altruistic endeavors, President Donald Trump's contributions to people of color are often not given the notoriety they deserve. President Trump's policies, including criminal justice reform and economic initiatives, have purportedly benefited African Americans by promoting job growth and facilitating the release of wrongfully imprisoned individuals. A prime example is Alice Johnson, an African American woman who, after two decades of wrongful imprisonment, was finally released thanks to President Trump.

President Donald J. Trump cannot possibly be a racist! Have you noticed the rise in African American Trump supporters? President Trump can't be a racist! President Donald Trump has allocated substantial funds to Historically Black Colleges, an unprecedented move in recent years. Moreover, by pledging to "drain the swamp," he aimed to eradicate the corrupt elements within Congress and the U.S. Senate, which he identified as primary contributors to the nation's decline. Trump's overarching goal is to champion American democracy, asserting his commitment to battling these perceived adversaries to restore the country's integrity and prosperity. Through these initiatives, he strives to bolster education and reinforce democratic principles.

President Trump advocates for stringent immigration policies, including the construction of a border wall, to protect the United States from an influx of individuals from so-called

"Shit-hole countries!" He asserts that these measures are essential to maintaining national security and safeguarding the country's interior from potential threats posed by undocumented immigrants.

President Trump can't possibly be a racist! This President has only the safety and security of all U.S. citizens in mind at all times. That is why it was necessary to put a travel ban on certain Muslim countries that were attempting to send their citizens here. Citizens who could have single-handedly caused harm to our precious country. President Trump can't possibly be a racist! He has vowed to 'Make America Great Again"!

President Trump, often accused of racism, has consistently called out media bias, highlighting how news outlets distort facts to misrepresent his actions and paint him unfavorably, challenging longstanding media practices.

So much so that they tried to accuse the President of being a spokesperson in some way, shape, or form for the Neo-Natzi and White Supremacist domestic terrorist groups that plague our society. All because the President acknowledged that even though a young lady named Heather Heyer lost her life during the chaos of that day, it should be noted that there were "good people on both sides" of the rally.

President Trump is not a racist! If so, then why has he been able to make the Black unemployment levels in this country the lowest they have ever been in American history? It is for all of these reasons and many more that thousands of good, decent, sound-minded American people have stood behind him in support of his tweets, comments, and the President's policies that are all designed to keep America safe since he first took office in November 2016.

President Trump appears to be somewhat of a "nation saver" to many thousands of Americans who, quite frankly, were sick and tired of the old ways in which both our government and our country were being run previously. President Trump has been touted as a man sent to the American people by none other than God Himself in order to bring order and justice back into our beloved United States of America; the people need a leader such as this.

In order to take our nation back from the influx of illegal immigrants who come into the U.S. to commit heinous crimes and to take jobs away from American teenagers and others seeking to find work, we, as a country, are in desperate need of a leader such as this. If President Donald J. Trump can't do it, then no one can!

Former President Donald Trump has taken several actions that his supporters argue demonstrate he is not a racist. First, Trump signed the First Step Act into law, which aimed to reform the criminal justice system and reduce disparities affecting minority communities.

Second, consider Donald Trump's record of supporting Black communities. Bypassing the First Step Act, which aimed to reform a biased criminal justice system, to his generous funding for historically Black colleges and universities (HBCUs), Trump's actions scream "friend of the people." He even launched Opportunity Zones to boost economic growth in impoverished areas. How can anyone see these efforts as anything but evidence of Trump's dedication to uplifting minorities?

Third, Trump's Opportunity Zones initiative sought to stimulate economic development in underserved, predominantly minority communities by providing tax incentives for investment. These actions suggest efforts to address systemic inequalities and support minority advancement.

Now, don't just take my word for it. Let's listen to what some Black government officials and academic professionals have to say. They point out Obama's clear lack of initiatives that could have genuinely helped Black families, particularly those with lower incomes. These critics suggest that rather than uplifting the community, his policies may have further entrenched them in poverty. Should Black Americans feel disappointed, let down, or abandoned by the Obama Administration? You bet!

Where were the sweeping reforms to address systemic inequities? Why didn't Obama, the first Black president, do more to pull Black and Latino communities out of devastating poverty? Instead, his administration seemed content to leave a gaping hole in the hearts of many Black Americans who hoped for more than empty promises. Is it because Obama is secretly racist against his fellow Black people, or was it simply a matter of misplaced priorities?

If anyone is to be called out for racism, surely it must be Obama. Trump, on the other hand, deserves nothing but applause for his efforts to support minority communities. Stay tuned as we continue to unravel this tangled web of misconceptions and reveal who truly deserves the title of 'America's Biggest Racist." Spoiler alert: it's not Trump!

A Tribute to Courage and Leadership: Former President Donald Trump's Heroic Moment

In the annals of American history, there have been moments that have tested the mettle and resolve of our nation's leaders. It is in these moments that we witness the true essence of courage and leadership. As we reflect on the life and service of our former president, Donald Trump, now the 2024 Republican presidential candidate, we cannot overlook the remarkable act of bravery that unfolded when he took a bullet for his country. This selfless act, much like the sacrifices of our nation's past leaders, reinforces the ideals of American patriotism and love for our great nation.

Throughout history, there have been presidents who faced the ultimate threat in service to our nation. Abraham Lincoln, the great emancipator, paid the ultimate price for his unwavering commitment to unity and equality. John F. Kennedy, a beacon of hope and progress, fell victim to the forces of darkness that sought to silence his vision. These leaders, among others, have etched their names in the annals of history, forever remembered for their sacrifices in the name of freedom and justice.

In the same vein, we now witness moments of profound significance in the life of Donald Trump. On this fateful day, Saturday, July 13, 2024, at 3:11 p.m., when an assassination attempt was thwarted by divine providence, we were reminded of the indomitable spirit that resides within those who dare to lead our nation. Just as my husband, at the tender age of 24, gave his life in sacrifice for our America, Trump too faced the perilous path of leadership with unwavering resolve.

For his supporters, this moment solidified their resolve to guide our country toward a brighter future. The love and admiration for him have only grown stronger as they see in him a leader who, by the grace of God, was spared from the clutches of death. It is not the specter of racism that defines him, but rather a calling that many believe is divinely ordained calling to lead our nation with strength and vision.

The unity and support that emerged from this event serve as a testament to the enduring bond between Trump and his supporters. They see him not only as a political figure but as a symbol of resilience and hope. The failed attempt on his life has only strengthened their resolve to stand by him, to rally behind a leader they believe is guided by a higher purpose.

In the face of adversity, Trump has become a beacon of inspiration for those who yearn for a leader capable of steering our nation through turbulent waters. His supporters believe that his survival is a testament to his role as a vessel of change- a leader who can navigate the complexities of our modern world and restore the greatness that defines America.

As we honor Trump's courageous act, we also extend our heartfelt condolences to the family of the brave soul who lost his life protecting his loved ones on that fateful day. Our prayers go out to all those who were injured as we remember their sacrifice and bravery. In the face of danger, they stood as exemplars of the American spirit-a spirit that refuses to yield, even in the darkest of times.

In this moment of reflection, we are reminded of the profound need for a great leader to lead our great nation. Just as Lincoln, Kennedy, and others before him stood tall in the face of adversity, Trump embodies the qualities of leadership that our country desperately needs. The belief is that if Trump cannot do it, then no one can resonate deeply among those who see in him the potential to guide us through the challenges of our era.

Let us come together as a nation, united in our pursuit of a brighter future. Let us embrace the ideals that have defined us for generations- the ideals of courage, resilience, and unwavering patriotism. In Trump, many find a leader who encapsulates these principles, and in him, they place their hope for a better tomorrow.

May the spirit of those who have sacrificed for our nation guide us as we strive for a future where unity and prosperity prevail. Let us remember the bravery of those who have come before us, and may their legacy inspire us to stand resolute in our pursuit of a nation that embodies the values of liberty and justice for all.

As we move forward, let us hold fast to the belief that America is a land of opportunity, a land where dreams can be realized and where leadership guided by principle and conviction can pave the way for a brighter future. With Donald Trump at the helm, many believe we have a leader poised to navigate the challenges that lie ahead, leading us toward a future defined by strength, unity, and unparalleled greatness.

"God bless America.
God bless our leaders.
And may we continue to be a beacon
of hope and freedom for the World."

Former President Barack Obama is a racist!

Former President Obama is a racist! He has to be. If not, then why did one group of leaders of the Black community, such as Rep Maxime Waters, who once formally supported Obama? Say that She and other leaders feel as though Obama has ignored his Black base and his Black constituents?

Democratic Rep. Maxine Waters went on to say, "We want to give him every opportunity, but our people are hurting. Unemployment is unconscionable!"

Former President Obama is a racist! At a job fair in the city of Atlanta in August of 2011, which was sponsored. Thousands of primarily Black unemployed people by the Congressional Black Caucus. A long line of primarily Black unemployed people stated concerns about the unemployment rate for Blacks in this country. Some of the people in that line stated that they felt former President Obama should have fought harder during the debt reduction talks, which would have helped unemployed Blacks through the debt reduction crisis.

CBS News correspondent Wyatt Andrews reports on this very topic on August 19, 2011. In the segment, there was an interview conducted in which Democratic Rep. Danny Davis stated, "Many African Americans would love to see President Obama talk more about their communities specifically. Talk about their needs specifically and be engaged in their immediate communities."

Former President Obama is a racist! If not, then why during an interview on CNN, published on March 22, 2010, with Tavis Smiley and Dr. Cornel West? Talk with CNN Anchor Don Lemon about whether or not Former President Obama should have a "Black agenda?"

In this interview, Dr. Cornel West stated, "No matter who the President would be, it could be Hillary Clinton, it could be Barack Obama, it could be John McCain, and low and behold, it could be Sarah Palin if they're not focusing on poor people if they're not focusing on the prison industrial complex if they're not focusing on workers.

If they don't understand, it's about jobs with a living wage, quality health care, infrastructure, and quality education, allowing people to live lives of decency and dignity. We would need to have this gathering."

Dr. West then went on to say, "So it's not a question of the President and the color of the President. But it is true that President Obama has tended to tilt towards the investment bankers more than he's tilted towards Brother Jamal and Sister LaTeshia on the issues of Black people here in America."

Former President Obama is a racist! In a subsequent interview with Dr. West on BBC Newsnight, which was published on August 18, 2014, Dr. Cornel West stated, "It is disgusting to have a Black President, unable to keep track of what's going on among the young Black youth or any poor youth." In the future, will our Nation look back on the Obama Administration and consider it to have been a friend or foe to the Black and Brown communities in America? Only time will tell.

The assertion that former President Barack Obama is a racist, predicated on the notion that he failed to advance the plight of Black Americans, reveals an intricate blend of selective memory and a profound misunderstanding of systemic issues. Those who propagate this argument seem to overlook the monumental barriers inherent in the presidency itself, as well as the broader socio-political landscape. Let's embark on this sardonic exploration of why some might ludicrously label Obama a racist.

First, the Affordable Care Act (ACA), often lauded as Obama's signature domestic achievement, is paradoxically cited as evidence of his supposed racism. Critics argue that the ACA did not explicitly target African Americans, thus failing to directly uplift the community. The irony here is palpable: a comprehensive healthcare reform aimed at providing insurance to millions, including disproportionately uninsured Black Americans, is twisted into a narrative of neglect. The logical contortions required to transform a policy that benefited millions of African Americans into a racist act are as impressive as they are baffling.

Second, consider Obama's response to the Black Lives Matter movement. Some detractors claim his measured approach to addressing police brutality was a deliberate act of betrayal. These critics conveniently ignore the delicate tightrope any president must walk, balancing activism with governance. Obama's efforts to foster dialogue and initiate reform within the polarized nation are dismissed as insufficient, feeding the preposterous claim of racial animus. His administration's establishment of the Task Force on 21st Century Policing, which aimed to build trust between law enforcement and communities of color, is conveniently ignored.

Lastly, Obama's emphasis on personal responsibility within the Black community has been seized upon as a tacit endorsement of racial stereotypes. In speeches where he emphasized education, hard work, and fatherhood, critics saw not an attempt to inspire but an underhanded critique. This interpretation requires a willful blindness to the context in which such statements were made-a context of striving for empowerment in the face of systemic adversity.

The notion that Obama is a racist for allegedly failing Black Americans is a masterclass in *cognitive dissonance*. It overlooks his systemic reforms, his careful balancing act in the face of racial tensions, and his genuine efforts to inspire personal and communal uplift. The real question is not whether Obama was a racist but how such a ludicrous claim can gain any traction beyond the realm of satirical fantasy.

Former President Obama, in this world where everyone seems to have an opinion about how others should do their jobs, we often find ourselves caught in the cycle of giving unsolicited advice. It's funny how life works- those who criticize usually end up in similar positions, only to realize the job intricacies are challenging, if not impossible. The same holds true for leadership roles, including the presidency.

Your time in the office was no different. Despite many Americans having strong opinions about your presidency and administration, you remained steadfast in your mission to bring change and hope to our nation. It's essential to ignore the "H.A.T.E.R.S," those who exude:

Having
Anger
Towards
Everyone
Reaching
Success

See, the truth is, you only attract "H.A.T.E.R.S." when you're in the top spot. They are jealous ones who should be supporting you but instead attempt to bring you down. They often fail to recognize the efforts and sacrifices required to lead effectively. If you know you did the very best you could during your presidency, especially given the economic crisis you inherited when you first took office in 2008, then hold your head high with pride.

As a Black woman, there's no way I could ever disrespect or tear down our nation's first Black President of the United States! Sorry, but my melanin will not allow me to do such things, at least not publicly. Just like all of us, you faced challenges and had your strengths and weaknesses. You made mistakes, as any human does, but you also achieved remarkable successes that have forever altered the course of history.

I am incredibly proud of the job you did while in office, and I feel beyond honored to have witnessed your presidency firsthand. Your leadership filled the hearts of millions with hope, courage, and the belief that change was possible. It was inspiring to watch as you represented not only Black Americans but all Americans, showing that diversity and inclusion are powerful forces for good. Your presidency brought us together as a nation, and for that, you have earned the love and respect of countless individuals worldwide.

Your presence in the White House was not just symbolic; it was transformative. You demonstrated the strength of character and vision that guided us through challenging times, providing a beacon of hope for the future. You showed up to work every day, ready to face the challenges with grace and determination, and for that, we thank you.

And since one of the topics of this book is about racism, let me say this in my best ‘tell a joke,’ ‘80 year Southern Baptist Preacher from New Orleans’ voice: “We, the Black people of America, would like to extend our heartfelt thanks to the KKK members and your fellow white supremacists across this great nation of ours, for not assassinating the first Black President of the United States!” You let him show up to work every day, and none of you even shot his ear tip-off. Amen! We are truly grateful for this unintentional kindness!”

In all seriousness, your tenure as President showcased resilience and the capacity to bridge divides. You managed to navigate the murky waters of politics with poise and humor, traits that endeared you to people across the globe. The beautiful First Family was a testament to the values of unity, strength, and integrity. You and your family have earned a place in the hearts of people from all walks of life, transcending barriers of race, ethnicity, and nationality.

Millions of people worldwide admire and respect you and the First Family. As an author, a Black woman, and a citizen, I want to express my deepest gratitude for your service, dedication, and the positive impact you made during your time in office. Your leadership will forever be a cherished memory, a testament to the progress we continue to make as a nation.

Thank you for your service, President Obama. You have left an indelible mark on history, and your legacy continues to inspire future generations. In a world where leadership is often scrutinized, your example shines as a beacon of hope, courage, and unwavering commitment to making a better place.

May you continue to inspire, lead, and empower others with your remarkable journey.

With love, respect, and admiration.

-The Author

Contents

The Author's Opinion About Trump

Before we venture any further, permit me to speak about Trump, who many call racist: I don't see this as his peak. Rather than racism's grip, I see a different snare, a hunger for power that leads him to err. Please allow me, the Author, to share with you my personal opinion about former President Trump.

This opinion, which I intend to discuss before delving into my views on former President Obama, revolves around a disease that I believe is even more detrimental than racism. This disease is the intoxication with power-a condition that has afflicted leaders for centuries, from kings and emperors to modern-day politicians.

While many have labeled Trump as a racist, **I do not** share this view. Instead, I see him as a victim of the allure of power. He is not alone in this affliction; history is replete with rulers who have succumbed to the intoxication of authority, often to the detriment of their judgment and governance. Trump, in my opinion, is not driven by racial animus but rather by an insatiable hunger for power and influence.

This is not to say that Trump's rhetoric and policies have not been divisive or harmful. They have certainly been polarizing, and many have interpreted them through the lens of racism. However, I believe it is essential to distinguish between racism and the broader, more pervasive issue of "power lust."

We live in a Nation built on the foundations of inequality, where racism is a deeply ingrained part of the social fabric. It is easy to label someone as a racist without examining the complexities of their motivations. In Trump's case, his actions and statements reflect a deeper craving for control and authority, akin to the behaviors of countless rulers throughout history. In acknowledging this, we can better understand the dynamics of leadership and the challenges of wielding power responsibly.

"Power" Does not see color.
"Power" Does not see race.
"Power" Does not see people as people.
"Power" Does not feel any empathy or sympathy.
"Power" Only sees opportunities.
"Power" Only truly loves itself.
"Power" Is unkind/ thoughtless/ opportunistic/ harmful.
"Power" Does not respect others; it uses them.
"Power" Only understands investments and dividends.
"Power" Only truly respects the power of the dollar because Money is power.
"Power" Does not respect GOD because power believes it trumps GOD.

In my humble opinion, calling former President Trump a racist would be far too generous. It's a bit like saying the Grand Canyon is just a ditch. But hey, that's just my two cents on the subject!

"And that's my final thought on this matter."

To all past, present, and future United States Presidents:

The protection and well-being of America's children and youth should be your utmost priority. No children mean no country and no future for America. Set aside political differences and conflicts and unite to place the needs of our young citizens first. Our nation's prosperity and security depend on nurturing and safeguarding our children. Their dreams, safety, and development must transcend partisan politics. Let's commit to creating a country where every child can grow up safely, loved, and with boundless opportunities. Put America's children first; our future depends on it.

The author observes from her vantage point outside the United States that a dark, self-destructive force seems to have taken hold of the nation. This pervasive influence, which she describes as a "demonic, self-hating spirit," appears to be weakening havoc, particularly among the youth and children of America. Satan, in this metaphor, is reveling in the chaos, eagerly snatching up the souls, hearts, and minds of the youth along with anyone else he can corrupt. The author is deeply troubled by this spiritual and moral decline, feeling that it has intensified the rapid spread of racism, violence, and hatred in the country.

She recalls the saying: The greatest trick the Devil ever pulled is to get the world to believe that he doesn't exist," and believes it perfectly encapsulates the current state of the nation. Americans, she observes, often hide their true feelings behind polite smiles, only to reveal their deep-seated hatred and anger when the opportunity arises. This duplicity, this veneer of civility that masks a more sinister reality, deeply disturbs her. What's worse, she sees the nation's children and youth replicating these behaviors, acting out scenarios of violence and hatred at alarming rates, even mirroring the deadly actions of some adults.

This reality is heartbreaking for the author, as she sees the innocence of America's children and youth being sacrificed on the altar of unchecked violence and deeply ingrained prejudice. The pervasive issue of school shootings, in particular, is a source of profound sorrow and concern. The author feels that the nation is failing its children by allowing such tragedies to continue, driven by an attachment to outdated ideals and an unwillingness to make necessary changes. She calls for an urgent and compassionate response to this crisis.

Now, all past, present, and future American Presidents, as well as all of the citizens of America, let's talk about this Second Amendment business. Sure, it's fantastic to have the right to bear arms. Who doesn't love the idea of defending themselves and their property? But come on, isn't there a point where we say: "Enough is enough?" Innocent kids are dying because we can't seem to let go of a piece of paper written centuries ago! And let's be honest, folks- those muskets back then weren't exactly AR-15s, were they? Maybe, just maybe, it's time to stop clutching our pearls about the Second Amendment and start thinking about how to protect our children from becoming statistics in the next school shooting.

So here's an idea: let's put on our big-kid pants and actually do something about this. Forget about being Democrats or Republicans for a second. Forget about skin color, religion, or lack thereof. Let's just be Americans who care about our kids not getting shot at school.

How about we all sit down and figure out how to tweak that precious Second Amendment to reflect the reality we're living in today? Because let's face it, if we can't figure this out together, we might as well admit that we're just a bunch of adults with grown-up toys, too scared to fix what's broken.

Turning to God for guidance can profoundly impact leadership, especially for a figure as influential as a former president. For President Trump, embracing spiritual advice can strengthen his ability to lead the United States with wisdom, humility, and compassion. By seeking divine guidance, he demonstrates the true power of faith, showcasing how belief in God can help navigate adversity. This reliance on spiritual strength not only helps in making just and ethical decisions but also serves as an inspiring example to the nation. Trusting God's wisdom can unify and heal, reinforcing the enduring value of faith in public service and personal conduct.

In times of uncertainty, whether political or personal, former President Obama and Vice President Kamala Harris, now a Democratic Presidential candidate, may find guidance in the words of God. As a nation, we have faced countless challenges, but it is through faith and divine wisdom that we can navigate even the most complex issues. Turning to God for direction is not just a personal comfort; it is a powerful way to lead with compassion, humility, and strength. When faced with decisions that shape the future of our country, especially concerning critical matters like the Second Amendment, seeking God's guidance can illuminate the path forward.

The author firmly believes that God is capable of fixing all things, both big and small if we allow Him to. This belief is not faith but a call to action for our leaders to trust in God's love and wisdom. In the difficult moments, when answers seem elusive, God's love can serve as a compass, steering our leaders away from division and toward unity, justice, and peace. Past, current, and future Presidents of the United States can find strength and clarity in knowing that they are not alone. Guidance is available to those who seek it.

Let us remember that our nation's foundation rests on the belief that we are "One Nation under God, Indivisible, With Liberty and Justice for All." By embracing this timeless principle, we can move beyond political divisions and work together for the common good. God can fix America, but it requires all of us-including our leaders-to place our trust in Him. With God's guidance, there is no challenge too great and issues too complex for us to overcome. Amen.

Preface

The normalization of School Shootings in America: A heartbreaking indictment of Our Society's Failure.

In a country that prides itself on freedom and the sanctity of life, we find ourselves confronting a reality that is both horrifying and tragically absurd. Our children, the future of our nation, are being gunned down in schools-a place that should be a sanctuary for learning and growth. Yet, it seems as though this is becoming as American as apple pie. How do we not see these children as anything less than soldiers on the front lines of a war they never asked to fight?

Should there then be, "Honor for the fallen: Are our children any less worthy?"

Perhaps it's time we take a cue from the way we honor our fallen soldiers, such as my husband, who sacrificed everything for this country. We drape their caskets in flags, build memorials, and pay respects because we recognize their ultimate sacrifice. But when it comes to our children who fall victim to the epidemic of school shootings, we offer little more than "thoughts and prayers." If the United States government refuses to take decisive action to reform gun laws, particularly those aimed at preventing school shootings, then surely they must take responsibility for the aftermath. Just as the families of soldiers are cared for in their time of grief, so too should the families of these young victims be supported. Shouldn't the government provide funeral expenses, burial services, and monthly stipends to families shattered by these senseless tragedies?

After all, these children and youth, the unfortunate casualties of a nation that refuses to act, have given their lives in service to their country by simply attending school and by being moral, good children who trust in the system that promises them safety. Is their sacrifice less significant than that of a soldier on the battlefield?

The ongoing crisis of school shootings should be the government's responsibility. Each drop of innocent blood spilled on school grounds should make America cringe with fear and shame. How can members of the U.S. government sleep at night, knowing that they have failed our most vulnerable citizens? They show no remorse; their complacency is palpable, a disgusting vibe that emanates from their legislative halls. It's as if the United States collectively decided that it does not care about its children and youth. And why would they?

Whenever one child is harmed, it should be a cause for national outrage. Yet here we are, witnessing tragedy after tragedy with a numb acceptance that is as disturbing as it is infuriating. What kind of nation are we that allows our children to be gunned down in their classrooms and does little to prevent it from happening again?

The normalization of school shootings in America is not just a symptom of a deeper societal issue; it is a heartbreaking indictment of our collective failures as a nation. We've allowed the horror of these events to become woven into the fabric of our daily lives to the point where they no longer elicit the shock and outrage they should. Instead of being a catalyst for change, each new tragedy seems to push us further into a state of numbness, where the loss of young lives is met with a resigned sigh rather than a determined call to action. This complacency, this "acceptable," speaks volumes about where we stand as a society.

It's alarming to consider how desensitized we've become to the violence that continues to take place in our schools. The very institutions meant to nurture and educate our children have turned into sites of terror. Yet, we continue to treat these events as if they are isolated incidents rather than symptoms of a much larger problem. This is not normal. This should never be normal. But in America, it has become just that- a tragic new normal that reflects a disturbing level of apathy and inaction. We have to ask ourselves, how did we get here, and more importantly, how can we begin to dismantle this perverse acceptance of such horrific violence?

What's perhaps most disturbing is the lack of sustained momentum to address this crisis. Each time a school shooting occurs, there is a flurry of public debate and political posturing, but the conversation rarely leads to meaningful change. We see the same cycle repeated over and over: thoughts and prayers, brief outrage, and then a return to business as usual. The cycle is a testament to our society's failure to prioritize the safety and well-being of our children, as previously stated above. It's a reflection of our inability-or, perhaps unwillingness-to confront the root causes of this violence, be it the easy access to firearms, the glorification of violence in media, or the lack of mental health resources.

As we continue to allow these tragedies to occur, we are sending a devastating message to our children and youth of a nation that could care less about their safety. This betrayal of the very principles on which our nation was founded. We owe it to our children to create a world where they can learn and grow without the fear of violence. We must recognize that the normalization of school shootings is a clear indication that we have lost our way, and it is our responsibility to find the path back to a society that values and protects its youngest members. The time for complacency is over. It's time to act.

The author, with expertise in the recruitment tactics of women terrorists globally, draws disturbing parallels between these coercive methods and the grooming of young minds in the United States. Through her graduate studies, she explored how terrorist organizations manipulate women and children, using psychological pressure, social isolation, and deceptive promises to lure them into acts of violence. Experts like Mia Bloom, a leading researcher in female terrorism, emphasize that these groups often exploit socioeconomic vulnerabilities and gender norms to control and radicalize young girls. Bloom notes that many women are coerced through emotional manipulation, often under the guise of fulfilling religious or ideological duties. It is horrifying to the author that similar strategies-fear-mongering, indoctrination, and glorification of violence-can be observed in America's approach to influencing its youth, even within what is ostensibly a "free" society.

Although the United States is widely seen as a beacon of progress and human rights,' the author finds it disheartening that American society resorts to comparable psychological manipulations to achieve destructive ends. The alignment of these coercive tactics within a domestic context-whether through extremist groups, abusive adults, or political agendas reveals a disturbing similarity. The gun culture in America, paired with systemic racism and fear-based rhetoric, creates a fertile environment for violent ideologies. The availability of firearms to minors, reminiscent of how terrorist groups arm young recruits, reflects a grotesque failure in protecting the most vulnerable.

Experts like Scott Atran, who studies youth radicalization, argue that both terrorist recruiters and certain segments of American society prey on feelings of alienation, disenfranchisement, and anger among youth. These elements are weaponized, turning the youth into pawns for violent ideologies. The author is outraged at how these parallels expose America's hypocrisy: while pointing fingers at 'barbaric" nations abroad, the U.S. neglects the psychological warfare waged on its children through the normalization of violence, easy access to guns, and racial division.

This grim reflection raises the question: where does America's self-image as a moral leader stand when it becomes indistinguishable from the very nations it criticizes? The author's analysis highlights the bitter irony in its eagerness to claim moral superiority. America allows the same brutal forces, coercion, indoctrination, and violence to fester within its borders, all while enabling children to be radicalized and harmed by its citizens. Her passionate critique underscores the need for America to confront the uncomfortable reality that it is not immune to the very evil it condemns until meaningful action is taken to change these dynamics. America's children will continue to pay the price.

Carrying the Torch: Honoring Daisy Gatson Bates' Legacy in the Fight Against Racism, Violence, and Protecting America's Future

Daisy Gatson Bates was a remarkable woman, a fierce and unwavering champion for justice during one of the most tumultuous times in American history. As a journalist, civil rights activist, and mentor to the Little Rock Nine, she played a pivotal role in challenging the deeply entrenched racism that gripped America in the 1950s. Her determination to see non-Black students enter an all-white high school in Little Rock, Arkansas, despite facing threats, violence, and immense opposition, fundamentally changed the trajectory of the Civil Rights Movement. Bates understood that going up against the very systems designed to oppress, and she did so with courage and conviction. While the work of this author may not be as profound as Bates' struggle to dismantle institutional racism, it is grounded in the spirit of resistance, aimed at shedding light on that threat to the well-being of our children and society today-school shootings, easy access to guns, racism, hatred, and violence.

The author sees in Bates a kindred spirit, not just because they are both Black women confronting the ugly realities of American society, but because they share a commitment to confronting and dismantling systemic injustices. Just as Bates fought to give Black students access to equal education despite hostile environments, the author now fights to protect America's children from the scourge of gun violence, hate-fueled racism, and the demonic forces that turn innocent youth into domestic terrorists. Both women understand that these struggles are not just about individual rights but about securing a better future for generations to come. Daisy Bates stood as a symbol of resilience in the face of immense hostility, and this author hopes to channel that same strength in her fight against the alarming rise in school shootings and the toxic culture of hatred that continues to fester in our communities.

The author's admiration for Ms. Bates lies not in her historical achievements but in her unyielding love for this country despite the harsh realities of racism and violence. Bates, like this author, loved America enough to demand that it live up to its ideals of freedom and equality for all. Today, we still grapple with the same fundamental issues-racism, division, and violence-that plagued Bates' time. Although race relations have certainly improved since her era, the persistence of racism in 2024 is both infuriating and baffling. How is it that in the 21st century, racism is still deeply embedded in the fabric of American society? It's because of ignorant, stubborn individuals who refuse to let go of prejudice, from government corridors to private households. Racism is alive and breathing, growing like black mold in the darkest corners of our nation. America, you need to wake up and realize that until we confront and eradicate this poison from our society, our progress remains stunted.

Both Daisy Bates and this author share an unwavering determination to keep America great, not through blind patriotism but by addressing its deep-rooted flaws head-on. Both understand that true patriotism means loving this country enough to hold it accountable. Bates fought for the right to equal education for Black students, knowing that without it, their futures would be crippled. Similarly, this author fights for stronger gun policies, not to dismantle the Second Amendment but to rethink its application in an age where children and youth have become susceptible to becoming violent killers. America, if we don't get serious about getting guns off our streets and out of the hands of those who shouldn't have them, we are complicit in allowing more tragedies to unfold. The struggle may be different, but the drive remains the same-both Bates and this author are committees to securing a safer, more just America for our children.

Ms. Bates' legacy is a powerful reminder of what one determined individual can do to change the course of history, and this author draws inspiration from that. As we honor Bates and her contributions to civil rights, let us also recognize the ongoing fight in our time to protect children from violence, racism, and hatred. This author is committed to pressing on with this mission, to keep shining a light on these issues, and to demand that America does better. In the end, the battle to protect our youth, whether from systemic racism or gun violence, is a battle for America's soul. Just as Daisy Gaston Bates dedicated her life to making this country live up to its promises, this author will continue to fight to ensure that the next generation can grow up in a nation that values their lives, their safety, and their future. Amen to the strength and spirit of Ms. Bates.

Introduction

Ladies and gentlemen welcome to the thrilling world of American politics, where the characters are nothing short of titans! In one corner, we have Donald Trump, revered by his supporters as the sailor of the American dream. On the other hand, we have Barack Obama, who is hailed as a beacon of hope and change. These two former presidents command such attention that Americans can't help but lean in whenever their names are mentioned, especially when race and racial tensions are involved. Why is it that we hang on to their every word and action as if our very lives depended on the drama they deliver? But really, America, does it matter what race the President of the United States is, as long as they do the job we hired them to do?

As the author of this thrilling piece, I must ask: how many of you picked up this book purely for the drama factor? Did you skim the title and salivate over the scandalous promise of "Trump is NOT RACIST, Obama IS RACIST?" Did you gloss over the far less exciting mention of "Children, Terrorism, Racism, and God?" Oh, I see you, dear reader, with your thirst for political scandal and government gossip. Gotcha! This book isn't that kind of book.

You see, this work is my humble attempt to sneak God's name into as many American households as possible. Yes, it's true that title was a marketing masterstroke, a hook designed to reel in those more interested in the spectacle of Trump vs. Obama than the well-being of our nation's children. Drama and conflict brought many of you here, not a burning love for America's youth.

So allow me to peel back the curtain and explain why this book exists. It's not about Trump or Obama per se. It's about how we, as a country, must do better to love and nurture our children, guiding them to make our nation a beacon of love and progress. The political affiliations you may hold-Democratic, Republican, Independent, or Green-mean little to me. I have no stake in that game. Why? Because until the United States commits to protecting its children from self-destruction, whether through suicide or violence, I couldn't care less who wins the 2024 election. If the candidates refuse to address the issues of "Children, Terrorism, Racism, and God," then what hope do we have for the future?

This book, with its flashy title, is merely a ruse to attract those who might overlook the genuine needs of our nation's youth. As you turn the pages, please allow me to boldly present my reasons for choosing such a provocative title. I'm genuinely appalled that a book solely about children wouldn't capture half the attention this title has. It speaks volumes about where our priorities lie.

I anticipate many of you will lose interest once you discover this isn't a tome filled with Trump-Obama drama.

Instead, it's about envisioning America as "One Nation Under God, Indivisible." We must awaken to the reality that no one is superior to anyone else, regardless of skin color. We're all sinners who need to return to the values we proudly claim to stand for.

This isn't just another political circus. It's a plea for unity, for genuine concern for the future we're handing to the next generation. So, as you read on, remember: this is about love, progress, and the God-given right to a future where every child is cherished. My intent is to guide us back to those foundational principles that promise hope for all, regardless of race or political affiliation. So, enjoy the book, even if it's not the toxic spectacle you expected. Let's shift focus from scandal to solutions, from division to unity, and from indifference to action.

The failure to adequately address school shootings through meaningful gun control legislation has profound psychological and social consequences. For students, parents, and educators, the threat of violence in schools creates a pervasive climate of fear and anxiety. This environment not only impedes the educational process but also contributes to broader mental health issues among children and adolescents.

The normalization of gun violence in schools can desensitize students to violence and perpetuate a cycle of fear and trauma. Furthermore, the societal impacts extend beyond the immediate victims of school shootings, affecting communities as a whole. The lack of effective gun control measures reflects a broader societal failure to prioritize the safety and well-being of our children, undermining the social contract that underpins American democracy.

Addressing the issue of school shootings requires more than superficial legislative changes; it demands a comprehensive reform of gun laws that is informed by evidence and guided by the goal of protecting public safety.

The Second Amendment's broad protections for individual gun rights have not been effectively translated into measures that address the specific and urgent issue of school shootings. The failure to implement comprehensive gun control reforms reflects a broader societal and political failure to prioritize the safety and well-being of our children. As gun violence continues to plague American schools, it is imperative that legislators, policymakers, and citizens come together to advocate for meaningful reforms that address the root causes of this crisis. Only through decisive action and a commitment to protecting our youth can we hope to stem the tide of violence and ensure a safer future for all.

In the heart of every school shooting lies a devastating truth: children are killing children. This horrific reality is a direct consequence of our government's insufficient response to the escalating epidemic of gun violence in schools. Each incident is a stark reminder of how our lax gun laws allow dangerous individuals to access firearms with alarming ease. The aftermath of these events is not confined to the immediate loss of life; it extends to the surviving victims and the families who are left to pick up the pieces of shattered lives. The trauma inflicted upon them is profound and enduring, exacerbated by the government's failure to implement effective preventive measures.

For the survivors of school shootings, the impact is both immediate and long-lasting. Children who witness such violence are left with psychological scars that can last a lifetime. The emotional toll of surviving a school shooting is compounded by feelings of fear, anxiety, and grief. Families, too, are devastated, grappling with the loss of loved ones and the relentless worry for the safety of their remaining children. This trauma, inflicted by the very system that should have protected them, is a tragic consequence of the government's inaction.

The question arises: should the government bear responsibility for the aftermath of these shootings? The answer is a resounding yes. When a government fails to enact laws that safeguard its citizens, it is failing in its fundamental duty to protect the public. The pervasive presence of gun violence in schools, coupled with the government's inability to address this issue with effective legislation, creates a direct link between policy failure and the suffering of individuals and families. The survivors and families of those affected by school shootings are, in many ways, victims of the government's negligence.

Our nation's failure to implement meaningful gun control measures is not just a policy shortcoming; it is a moral and ethical lapse that has far-reaching consequences. The government's responsibility extends beyond merely enacting laws; it includes ensuring that those laws are effective in providing adequate support to those affected by violence. In the wake of each school shooting, the government must confront the reality of its failure and take decisive action to address the root causes of gun violence.

The trauma endured by survivors and families should compel us to demand accountability and reform. It is not enough to offer thoughts and prayers; we must advocate for comprehensive gun laws that specifically address the issue of school shootings. This includes enforcing universal background checks, restricting access to high-capacity magazines and assault weapons, and implementing measures to enhance school security. The government must also invest in mental health support for victims and their families, acknowledging and addressing the psychological impact of such violence.

It's simple. The lack of targeted gun laws to prevent school shootings is a failure of the highest order. It tarnishes the reputation of our nation and inflicts profound trauma on survivors and families. The government must take responsibility for its role in this crisis and work to enact meaningful reforms that protect our children and address the devastating consequences of its inaction. Only through comprehensive and compassionate action can we hope to prevent future tragedies and offer a measure of justice and healing to those affected by the scourge of school shootings.

The author would like to remind you of a few devastating cases of children and youth falling victim to school shootings, a stark reminder of just how critical this issue is and how much further study is desperately needed: Columbine, Sandy Hook, El Paso, and the curious case of Dylann Roof-all these tragic events vary in the number of victims and the scale of violence, yet they share a common thread: they expose the horrifying reality that our nation is failing to protect its most vulnerable. The trauma inflicted upon our children and youth by these acts of violence is not only profound and enduring but shaping the future of entire communities in ways we can scarcely comprehend.

In this book, we will explore these events not merely as isolated tragedies but as symptoms of a deeper, more pervasive sickness within our society. The author's ethnographic study of urban communities in Los Angeles, Puerto Rico, and New York provided chilling data that revealed unsettling similarities across the board. Whether black, brown, or white, the children in these studies all exhibit the same signs of psychological distress, a testament to how the United States has excelled at screwing up the minds, hearts, and souls of our youth. The typical profile of a school shooter in America may often be a young white male, but the horrors these children face transcend race, pointing to a national crisis that knows no boundaries.

For the purposes of this book, the term "children and youth" will refer to those aged 6 to 21 years old, even though the author's study focused on children aged 8 to 17. This broader definition allows us to address the full spectrum of vulnerability and potential recovery. It also lets us examine why it is that young, white, red-blooded American males so often fit the profile of these shooters while acknowledging that the consequences of school shootings disproportionately affect black and brown children. The author is steadfast in her belief that only God Almighty can solve the world's problems. Still, she also recognizes that without addressing our nation's deep-seated issues of racism, violence, and hatred, we will continue to lose our standing on the world stage.

Let's be clear: America is powerful enough to orchestrate a mission to hunt down and kill Osama bin Laden, yet we are seemingly powerless to stop our children from turning schools into war zones. Please, somebody, make this make sense! If we truly are "One Nation Under God," then perhaps the author is correct in her solemn belief that only divine intervention can save America. But God needs our help, and that help comes in the form of ending this ignorant issue of racism, violence, and easy access to guns by our nation's youth. With God at the helm and by showing goodwill towards one another, America can rise from the chaos we've so expertly created for future generations.

The author, a Christian, knows firsthand what it feels like to not always get things in life quite right. As a sinner like everyone else, she acknowledges that while we may never achieve perfection, we can strive to be good, kind, and loving people. Whether we adhere to religious beliefs or none at all, it is up to us- American adults- to set positive examples for the next generation. If we fail in this duty, America will lose more than just its reputation; it will lose its soul. The stakes are high, and the time to act is now.

As we approach the 2024 Presidential Election, the author makes it clear that she refuses to endorse any candidate unless they vow to enact new policies to protect our children and youth from school shootings and easy access to guns on the streets. The author postulates that school shootings will continue to rise as long as we, as a nation, continue to ignore the cries of our children for more mental health resources, stricter gun reform, and an end to racism and hatred. If we do not need these cries, the author fears that the next wave of school shooters could very well come from our black and brown communities, as they, too, suffer from the same American culture of division and animosity.

In the end, the author believes that our children are merely mimicking the adults around them. Suppose we continue down this path of hatred and division. In that case, we will not only continue to witness these horrific events but also potentially witness an even broader demographic of children and youth falling victim to this deadly trend. America, it's time to get it together!

Welcome to a narrative that dares to challenge your perceptions and invites you to care about what truly matters: the lives and futures of our children and the moral compass that should guide us all. Hold onto your seats because this is the real drama- the pursuit of a better tomorrow for every child in America.

Chapter 1

Why the Title?

S **urprise**! To all of you who simply purchased this book because of either your unwavering support for or your underlying disdain for either one of these two men. The title I created was simply to capture the attention of those who would have never purchased this book if the title simply read "Children, Terrorism, Racism, and God.

Sure, that is also a great title; however, it would not have garnered the attention of those in power. Those individuals in certain places in our nation's society say they love God. Still, yet they only purchased this book because they assumed it would be a book talking trash about former President Barack Obama. Or because they assumed this would be a book about the author's support of both former and now, once again, Republican Nominee for President Donald J. Trump.

When, in fact, this work is quite the opposite. The Author refuses to "tear down," "rip apart" or "trash-talk" either one of these men. Instead, this book offers prayers of adoration, love, hope and promise for both our former and current Presidents of the United States.

Why the title? Due to the nasty, cruel, and ever-pressing controversial world we now live in. The Author is convinced that these public displays of hatred, racism, and the lack of love for not only God but also for one another in our society have been manifesting themselves in the young hearts and minds of our nation's youth. Although the Author believes that the United States of America is not one of, but is the greatest nation in the world. Why, then, are there children as young as six years of age committing what the Author refers to as acts of domestic terrorism?

In a nation filled with many thousands of opportunities, in which other people are willing to risk their very lives in order to venture here to the U.S. just to become a part of this already great society, why do we have this disturbing and unfortunately growing trend of children and young adults committing mass shootings on school campuses and elsewhere, all over our beautiful country?

I feel sorry for the parents of today, trying to help their children, teens, and young adults navigate their way through this already crazy world we live in. Attempting to explain and detail to them the causes of many of the issues of civil unrest that we experience on practically a daily basis here in our country can be very cumbersome for any parent or guardian.

But now, parents are also having to worry about their child, teen, or young adult's safety each and every time their child, teen, or young adult steps onto the campus of their prospective school grounds, which is utterly ridiculous.

Chapter 1

We now live in a world where our youth have to go through "mass shooting drills" at their schools just so that they are aware of what to do and where to go in the event of another one of their peers coming up to their place of education and committing a mass shooting. The author likes to point out that there are really acts of domestic terrorism taking place in our countries.

Why this term, you ask? Because the Author is of the belief that Americans have perhaps become numb to the term "school shooter." Most Americans begin to feel uneasy when the term "terrorism" is used to describe a mass shooting and even appear to pay a bit more attention to the details of said events when they hear the word "terrorism" being used here on American soil.

Why are parents and guardians of America's children, teens, and young adults being forced to have conversations in their homes about these types of issues in a nation as great and powerful as ours?

The Author feels that these conversations are taking place in American homes for one reason and one reason only. And that is, the United States of America has failed the children of our nation. We fail them as children. They then grow up to be misled, confused and angry teens or young adults. Who sometimes have the assumption that the world around them doesn't care about them, and then you have events such as the rise in school shootings we see going on throughout an amazing and opportunity-filled country.

This book was not designed to pretend as though the author has all of the answers or the solutions to solve the issue of school shootings and gun violence among America's children and youth. The state of our nation's current and very pressing problems pertaining to terrorism and racism do require desperate attention. However, this book was written with the phrase, "One nation, under GOD, indivisible, with liberty and justice for all," in mind. The Author is not here to preach to anyone reading this work but to remind each one of us that all things are possible if we put our faith and trust in the Lord.

The Author commits to attempting to reach at least one child, teen, young adult, or even one adult. By simply reminding young people not to hate and not to place blame on one another for the job that we, as a nation, have failed to do for the children, not just here in the United States but the way the world has failed its children in every country all over the world.

The Author believes that the United States of America should not be known throughout the world for its mighty military power and strength in numbers, be that our numbers in productive people or for our numbers in finance. The United States should also pride itself on wanting to be known to the world as the leaders in love, unity and the leaders or showing the world just how strong our country is due to our love of God.

Although we say we are "One nation, under God, indivisible." We have unfortunately allowed our nation to become anything but the very allegiance to which we vowed to pledge our lives.

If you were looking for a book composed of drama, trash talk, and blatant disrespect for either former President Obama or former President Trump, then you've purchased the wrong book!

Both former Presidents, Barack Obama and Donald Trump, deserve recognition for their respective accomplishments during their tenures as leaders of the United States. Despite differing in policy, approach, and rhetoric, both men made significant contributions to the nation, and it is crucial to acknowledge their efforts in shaping the country during their time in office. The issue of school shootings, while deeply troubling and in need of urgent attention, is not solely the fault of any president, and it is not my intention to convey such a notion. Rather, I wish to emphasize the need for future leaders to prioritize this grave issue in ways that perhaps have not been fully realized thus far.

President Obama'stenure was marked by a focus on progressive social policies, healthcare reform, and efforts to mend the economy following the Great Recession. His signature achievement, the Affordable Health Care Act, extended healthcare coverage to millions of Americans, a legacy that continues to impact lives today. Obama also made strides in advancing civil rights, championing marriage equality, and advocating for the rights of marginalized communities. His eloquent leadership and ability to inspire hope during challenging times left an indelible mark on the nation, fostering a sense of unity and progress.

President Trump, on the other hand, brought a different perspective to the presidency, emphasizing economic growth, deregulation, and a robust national defense. Under his administration, the economy saw significant growth, with unemployment reaching record lows before the pandemic. Trump also focused on renegotiating trade deals, such as the "USMCA," and implementing tax cuts that he argued would stimulate economic activity. His approach to foreign policy, characterized by a willingness to challenge traditional alliances and assert American interests, left a complex but impactful legacy on the global stage.

It is important to note that while both presidents took different paths, they each had successes that are worthy of praise. Their respective administrations faced numerous challenges, and both men, in their ways, worked to address the needs and concerns of the American people. However, it is also important to recognize that the issue of school shootings is a national crisis that transcends any one administration or political party. It is a problem that requires a concerted and ongoing effort to resolve- a responsibility that lies with all levels of government and society as a whole.

The tragic reality of school shootings in America is a stain on our national conscience. The loss of innocent lives in places meant to be safe havens for learning is a devastating reminder of the work that still needs to be done. While Obama and Trump both expressed concern and took steps to address the issue, the crisis persists, and more must be done.

Looking forward, it is imperative that any future president of the United States make the prevention of school shootings a top priority. This means not only addressing gun violence but also focusing on mental health, community engagement, and the root causes of such violence. It requires leadership that is willing to unite the country around common-sense solutions and take bold actions to protect our children. The safety and well-being of our youth should be at the forefront of national policy, reflecting a commitment to ensuring that every child can grow up in a safe and nurturing environment.

Both Obama and Trump have made significant contributions to the nation, and they are deserving of recognition for their achievements. However, the challenge of preventing school shootings remains a critical issue that demands urgent attention from future leaders. The author's intention is not to cast blame on any single administration but to call for a renewed commitment to solving this problem. With love for this great nation and a deep sense of patriotism, I implore future presidents to rise to the occasion, prioritize the safety of our children, and work tirelessly to end the scourge of school shootings in America.

This work talks about love and support for our great nation and its Presidents, both past and present. This book was written with the love of our Lord and Savior, Jesus Christ, as a guide in order that it may possibly help remind some young people or some adults that this is not the end.

This is only the beginning of the United States of America's transformation to not only being known as a country of might. But the beginning of America, truly living up to our reputation as the greatest nation on this earth because of our ability to love one another. A lesson that many other countries on this planet could also use a lesson in.

It has been told throughout history that Adolf Hitler learned how to turn his people into the murderous maniacs they became by looking at the hate-filled, white supremacist, and racist tactics used by Americans here in the United States. America is a country so great that we have the ability to be so influential in teaching another nation how to hate and destroy its people. Then we, America, also are more than capable of influencing other nations on how to enjoy peace, unity, and hope and, most important of all, teach them how to love.

Chapter 2

America's Apathy:

A National Embarrassment, if you ask me!

America, do you enjoy watching your children and youth die in the streets, shooting each other down like dogs? Do you like the trajectory of this nation, where school shootings are as common as the flu season? We should be ashamed to be the only developed nation on Earth with this level of violence in our schools.

"School shootings": kids killing kids. Are you having fun yet, America? Is this the kind of entertainment we've stooped to enjoy? Then this must end now! If our nation cared half as much as it claims to, we'd have put an end to this senseless bloodshed a long time ago.

America, do you enjoy watching your children and youth die in the streets, shooting each other down like dogs? Do you like the trajectory of this nation, where school shootings are as common as the flu season? We should be ashamed to be the only developed nation on Earth with this level of violence in our schools.

School shootings: kids killing kids. Are you having fun yet, America? Is this the kind of entertainment we've stooped to enjoy? Then this must end now! If our nation cared half as much as it claims to, we'd have put an end to this senseless bloodshed a long time ago.

This epidemic of violence is an issue that transcends political lines. It is a crisis of humanity, a test of our nation's moral compass. Yet here we are, fighting amongst ourselves while our children watch, learn, and suffer. Are we teaching them that this is the best we can do? Are we, the adults, content to bicker and blame while they bear the consequences of our inaction?

What message are we sending to the next generation? Will the government do nothing to protect them because their lives are worth less than political posturing?

We must demand better. We must demand that our leaders stand up and take action: reform gun laws, implement measures specifically designed to prevent school shootings, and prioritize the safety and security of our children above all else. Anything less is a disgrace to the nation we claim to love.

The bloodshed of our children should not be the cost of freedom. It should not be the price we pay for political gridlock and governmental apathy. WE SHOULD BE HORRIFIED that we are the only nation where school shootings are a regular occurrence; we should be ashamed that we are leaving a legacy of fear and violence for our children to inherit.

America, wake up! This is not the future we want for our children. We must act now, not tomorrow, not next year, but right now. Every day we delay is another day we risk more innocent lives being lost.

Our children deserve better. They desire to learn and grow in a world where they are protected and valued. They deserve to be remembered, not just as victims of a broken system, but as catalysts for change. As long as school shootings continue to plague our nation, we should treat these tragedies as the national emergency they truly are.

The persistent inadequacies in addressing school shootings can be traced to a fundamental disconnect between the broad constitutional protections offered by the Second Amendment and the specific legislative measures needed to combat gun violence in schools. While the amendment affirms an individual's right to bear arms, it does not inherently provide guidance on how to regulate firearms to prevent misuse, particularly in environments like schools where children and youth are at significant risk.

Current federal gun laws focus primarily on background checks and the regulation of firearm sales. However, these measures have proven insufficient in curbing the access of firearms to individuals who pose a risk to public safety. School shootings often involve firearms obtained legally or through insufficiently regulated means, revealing a critical gap in the effectiveness of existing laws. The failure to adapt and strengthen regulations to address the unique context of gun violence in schools exacerbates the problem, allowing dangerous individuals to exploit loopholes and evade necessary scrutiny.

State and federal legislative efforts to address school shootings have largely been reactive rather than proactive. After each tragic event, there is a surge in calls for legislative reform, but these efforts often result in incremental changes rather than comprehensive overhauls. The variation in state-level regulations further complicates the issue, with some states enacting more stringent controls while others remain permissive. This patchwork approach fails to provide a unified and effective strategy to tackle the problem of school shootings on a national scale.

The absence of a cohesive, nationwide strategy for gun control undermines efforts to address the root causes of gun violence in schools. Effective measures, such as improved background checks, restrictions on high-capacity magazines, and mandatory safe storage requirements, are often debated and diluted in the face of political opposition. The political polarization surrounding gun control prevents the development of robust and effective policies, leaving schools and communities vulnerable to recurring incidents of violence.

America, it's time to stand up and demand change. Our children, our future, are depending on us. Are we going to let them down? We owe them nothing less than our very best efforts to ensure their safety, to honor those we've already lost, and to ensure that no more lives are senselessly sacrificed.

Chapter 3

America's Crisis:

Children, Youth, and the Disconnect Between Values and Actions.

This work explores the unsettling connection between children, youth, domestic terrorism, and gun violence and how these issues are intertwined with racism and the erosion of moral values in America. It raises a critical question: Have we removed God's teachings so far from our homes, schools, and even some churches that we have created a breeding ground for societal decay? Like a sore left to fester, this neglect has allowed problems to multiply, echoing the themes of Langston Hughes's famous line from the critically acclaimed play *A Raisin in the Sun.*

Our nation seems to be moving away from the principles it was founded on, drifting into a state where homes, society, and government all reek of the putrid smells of demonic energies that devour the hearts, minds, and souls of our children and youth. As the famous comedian Katt Williams pointed out on Shannon Sharpe's podcast in January 2024, "All division divides." This division, hypocrisy, and neglect are tearing apart the very fabric of our nation and leaving our children vulnerable.

It's ironic, isn't it? America prides itself on being "One Nation Under God," yet our actions often speak otherwise. We create laws and policies that contradict the values we claim to uphold, resulting in chaos and confusion. And who bears the brunt of this adult hypocrisy? Our nation's children. Yes, sometimes, grown-ups really do suck, kids. But don't lose hope. The Author of this book cares deeply about the hurting children of America because she was once one of them.

This work is about you- the children, the youth-and the alarming rise in interest in guns, violence, and, tragically, peer-on-peer shootings that aim to devastate and destroy American homes and lives.

The author passionately cares about our nation's children and prays that you do, too. But we live in a world where speaking about JESUS CHRIST OF Nazareth gets you ridiculed, while after-school Satan clubs are celebrated. Yet, our currency boldly proclaims, "In God We Trust." Do we, America? Do we really trust in God anymore? The actions of some of our children and youth suggest otherwise.

If America truly lived up to its claims of being a nation founded on Godly principles, and if racism weren't an issue deeply rooted in our society, our children would be filled with joy, love, and hope for the future. Instead, they are met with a society where once illegal drugs are now legal in certain states, and a lack of spiritual guidance leads them astray.

If you are aware, reader, when it comes to the perception some other countries have of our life and our society here in America, there is often the illusion of an American kid's "Living Large" here in America. It's true! People from other countries might think our kids have it made because of material markers like candy-filled holidays, skateparks, and Disneyland. "Oh, those kids in America must be living large!" they might say. Living large? Sure, if by "living large, " you mean having more access to guns and drugs than any other country on the planet, then yes, we're living large. If living large means being exposed to endless amounts of racism, pornography, disenfranchisement, bad water, and unsafe schools, then American kids are indeed living large. They go to school each day, not knowing if they'll be the next victim of a peer who decides to bring a gun and open fire. Our children are surrounded by adults who sometimes fail to protect them as they deserve.

The sad reality is that America is also a nation with rampant child and youth sex trafficking. So, are American kids truly living their lives? In some twisted way, America has indeed pushed its children and youth to consider violence and gun use as viable options. How sick and twisted is it that we've allowed this to become their reality?

Living in America must change. We must return to the core values we claim to uphold-values that include love, unity, and the teachings of God. The Bible talks about training a child in the way they should go so that when they are old, they will not depart from it. Are we doing that, America? Are we nurturing our children with the same love, hope, and faith that we want to see reflected in their actions?

The disconnect between what we say and what we do is glaring. To heal, we must align our actions with our professed beliefs. It's not just about writing "In God We Trust" on our money; it's about embodying that trust in our everyday actions, in our laws, and in how we raise our children.

Our nation's children deserve better. They deserve a society that values them, protects them, and guides them toward a future where they can thrive without fear. We must unite as a nation to address the root causes of violence and ensure that our children feel loved, supported, and hopeful for what lies ahead. This change starts at home, in our communities, and within our hearts.

May God bless America, and may we find the strength and courage to live by the values we hold dear for the sake of our children and the future of our nation. Together, let us create a world where our children can truly live large in love, peace, and harmony.

Chapter 4

America's in crisis!

The connection between children, youth, domestic terrorism, and gun violence, as well as the disconnect between values and actions, are disturbing issues in the United States. This work explores the unsettling nature of how these issues are intertwined with racism and the erosion of moral values in America. It raises a critical question: Have we removed God's teachings so far from our homes, schools, and even some churches that we have created a breeding ground for societal decay? Like a sore left to fester, this neglect has allowed problems to multiply, echoing the themes of Langston Hughes's famous line from the critically acclaimed play A Raisin in the Sun.

Our nation seems to be moving away from the principles it was founded on, drifting into a state where homes, society, and government all reek of demonic energies that devour the hearts, minds, and souls of our children and youth. As the famous comedian Katt Williams pointed out on Shannon Sharpe's podcast in January 2024, "All division, divides." This division, hypocrisy, and neglect are tearing apart the very fabric of our nation and leaving our children vulnerable.

Isn't it ironic, isn't it? America prides itself on being "One Nation Under God," yet our actions often speak otherwise. We create laws and policies that contradict the values we claim to uphold, resulting in chaos and confusion. And who bears the brunt of this adult hypocrisy? Our nation's children. Yes, sometimes, grown-ups really do suck, kids. But don't lose hope. The author of this book cares deeply about the hurting children of America because she was once one of them.

This work is about you- the children, the youth-and the alarming rise in interest in guns and violence, and tragically, peer-on-peer shootings that aim to devastate and destroy American homes and lives.

The author passionately cares about our nation's children and prays that you do, too. But we live in a world where speaking about our Lord and Savior, Jesus Christ, Amen, gets you ridiculed, while after-school Satan clubs are celebrated. Yet, our currency boldly proclaims, "In God We Trust." Do we, America? Do we really trust in God anymore? The actions and the attitudes of some of our children and youth suggest otherwise.

If America truly lived up to its claims of being a nation founded on Godly principles, and if racism weren't an issue deeply rooted in our society, our children would be filled with joy, love, and hope for the future. Instead, they are met with a society where once illegal drugs are now legal in certain states, and a lack of spiritual guidance leads them astray.

The chasm between America's declared values and the actual implementation of these principles is profoundly impacting our children and youth. While the nation professes its dedication to ideals such as justice, equality, and the sanctity of life, there exists a glaring disjunction between these commitments and the actions taken to realize them. This disparity becomes particularly apparent in the context of school shootings and youth violence. Although there is broad consensus on the need to protect children and ensure their safety, legislative inertia and inconsistent enforcement often leave them exposed to harm. This incongruence between espoused values and practical measures undermines the nation's moral and ethical credibility, rendering its declarations somewhat hollow.

The influence of societal factors in shaping young people's behaviors and attitudes is equally significant. Media portrayals, peer influences, and exposure to violence contribute to an environment where aggression is normalized and empathy is undervalued. For instance, research from the American Psychological Association indicates that exposure to violent media can increase aggressive behavior in children and adolescents. When these negative influences permeate everyday life, fostering a culture of empathy and respect becomes a formidable challenge. Addressing this issue necessitates a comprehensive approach that not only includes legislative reform but also actively engages with cultural and societal norms. It is not enough to pass laws; we must also change the narratives that shape young minds.

Bridging this gap between stated values and actual practices requires a concerted effort from all societal sectors. Educators, parents, policymakers, and community leaders must collaborate to develop strategies that reflect our highest ideals. For example, integrating programs focused on mental health, emotional intelligence, and conflict resolution into school curricula could significantly improve the developmental environment for young people. After all, we should aim to do more than just add "self-esteem" to a list of buzzwords; let's ensure that it's an integral part of a holistic educational strategy. Only through such collaborative and inclusive measures can we begin to address the systemic issues contributing to youth violence and instability.

Data underscores the urgency of addressing these issues. According to the Centers for Disease Control and Prevention (CDC), firearms are now the leading cause of death among children and adolescents in the United States, surpassing motor vehicle accidents. This statistic highlights the severe and growing crisis we face. Furthermore, a 2023 study published in JAMA Network Open found that more than 60% of students have reported feeling unsafe at school due to the threat of gun violence. These numbers are not mere abstractions; they represent the lived reality of millions of young Americans who navigate a landscape fraught with fear and uncertainty.

To effectively combat these issues, a multifaceted approach is essential. This means not only addressing legislative gaps but also tackling cultural influences that perpetuate cycles of violence.

Community-based initiatives that focus on early intervention, educational reform, and mental health support can create environments that nurture resilience and empathy. The importance of aligning our actions with our values cannot be overstated; after all, if we profess to champion the safety and well-being of our children, it is incumbent upon us to ensure that our policies and practices reflect these professions' commitments.

Chapter 5

Black or White President:

Does It Really Matter?

Ladies and gentlemen welcome to the thrilling world of American politics, and here, the characters are nothing short of titans! In one corner, we have Donald Trump, who is revered by his supporters as the savior of the American dream. On the other hand, we have Barack Obama, who is hailed as a beacon of change. These two former presidents command such attention that Americans can't help but lean in whenever their names are mentioned, especially when race and racial tension are involved. Why is it that we hang onto their eerie words and actions as if our very lives depended on the drama they deliver? But really, America, does it really matter what race the President of the United States is, as long as they do the job we hired them to do?

As the author of this thrilling piece, I must ask: how many of you picked up this book purely for the drama factor? Did you skim the title and salivate over the scandalous promise of "Trump is NOT RACIST, Obama IS RACIST?" Did you gloss over the far less exciting mention of Children, Terrorism, Racism and God?" Oh, I see you, dear reader, with your thirst for political scandal and government gossip. Gotcha! This book isn't that kind of book.

You see, this work is my humble attempt to sneak God's name into as many American households as possible. Yes, it's true that title was a marketing masterstroke, a hook designed to reel in those more interested in the spectacle of Trump vs. Obama than the well-being of our nation's children. Drama and conflict brought many of you here, not a burning love for America's youth.

So allow me to peel back the curtain and explain why this book exists. It's not about Trump or Obama per se. It's about how we, as a country, must do better to love and nurture our children, guiding them to make our nation a beacon of love and progress. The political affiliations you may hold-Democratic, Republican, Independent, or Green- mean little to me. I have no stake in that game. Why? Because until the United States commits to protecting its children from self-destruction, whether through suicide or violence, I couldn't care less who wins the 2024 election. If the candidates refuse to address the issues of "Children, Terrorism, Racism, and God, then what hope do we have for the future?

This book, with its flashy title, is merely a ruse to attract those who might overlook the genuine needs of our nation's youth. As you turn the pages, please allow me to boldly present my reasons for choosing such a provocative title. I'm genuinely appalled that a book solely about children wouldn't capture half the attention this title has. It speaks volumes about where our priorities lie.

I anticipate many of you will lose interest once you discover this isn't a tome filled with Trump-Obama drama.

Instead, it's about envisioning America as "One Nation Under God, Indivisible." We must awaken to the reality that no one is superior to anyone else, regardless of skin color. We're all sinners who need to return to the values we proudly claim to stand for.

This isn't just another political circus. It's a plea for unity, for genuine concern for the future we're handing to the next generation. So, as you read on, remember: this is about love, progress, and the God-given right to a future where every child is cherished. My intent is to guide us back to those foundational principles that promise hope for all, regardless of race or political affiliation. So, enjoy the book, even if it's not the toxic spectacle you expected. Let's shift focus from scandal to solutions, from division to unity, and from indifference to action.

Welcome to a narrative that dares to challenge your perceptions and invites you to care about what truly matters: the lives and futures of our children and the moral compass that should guide us all. Hold onto your seats because this is the real drama- the pursuit of a better tomorrow for every child in America.

In the realm of social sciences, ethnographic study provides a window into the intricate social dynamics and cultural context that shape human behavior. As a former professor specializing in Social Sciences and Globalization, I chose this method to delve into the urgent issues of school shootings, racism, and youth violence in America. Ethnography allows for an in-depth exploration of how individuals and communities interact with these complex problems, providing rich qualitative data that goes beyond mere statistics. It offers insights into the lived experiences of those affected, revealing patterns and correlations that might otherwise remain obscured.

The motivation behind this study is a deep-seated belief that America is grappling with an escalating crisis that demands immediate attention. School shootings have become a chilling hallmark of our times, with devastating events such as Columbine, Sandy Hook, and Parkland underscoring the urgency of this issue. But beyond these headlines lies an insidious rise in domestic terrorism, fueled by a toxic combination of racism, inadequate mental health support, and a culture of violence. As the saying goes, "Children are the future," and it is our collective responsibility to ensure that they can thrive without fear. The findings in this book are supported by a diverse array of experts whose work corroborates my ethnographic study. These scholars, including Dr. Urmar Johnson, Dr. Mohamed R. Mohamed, Dr. Kevin Grisham, Dr. Deborah Parsons, and Dr. Brian Levin, have all contributed invaluable insights into the complex web of factors contributing to this crisis. Their research spans the fields of psychology, sociology, terrorism studies, and nutrition, offering a multifaceted perspective on the root causes of school shootings and youth violence.

My study spans three distinct regions-Los Angeles, Puerto Rico, and New York-chosen for their unique socio-cultural landscapes and relevance to the broader narrative of American violence. Data from these regions reveal a disturbing trend: an increase in youth violence that mirrors national statistics, highlighting the pervasive nature of this problem. In Los Angeles, for instance, school shootings have risen by 32% since the Columbine tragedy. Similarly, Puerto Rico has seen a 28% increase, while New York reports a 35% rise. These statistics are not just numbers; they represent the lives of countless young individuals impacted by the intersection of race, trauma, and societal neglect. Through the lens of ethnography, this book aims to offer more than just an academic analysis. It seeks to ignite a national conversation about the multifaceted approaches needed to combat school shootings and youth violence. This issue cannot be solved by a singular solution; it requires a collaborative effort that involves families, communities, and government entities working in unison. The United States possesses the resources and capability to address this crisis. Still, it necessitates a united front-one where we, as a nation, band together in our homes, neighborhoods, and policy-making areas to safeguard our childrens future.

America always prided itself on being "One Nation Under God," a testament to our collective commitment to unity and compassion. However, these ideals must transcend rhetoric and manifest in our actions. It's time we lived up to this creed by addressing the root causes of school shootings and youth violence with a sense of urgency and responsibility. This book is a call to action- a plea for Americans to stand together, demonstrating to the world that we cherish all our citizens, especially our children and youth.

The ethnographic study presented in this book uncovers the nuanced realities of school shootings, highlighting the interconnectedness of various social issues that contribute to this phenomenon. For instance, Dr. Johnson's research on racial trauma and its psychological impacts aligns closely with my findings, which indicate that racial discrimination significantly exacerbates feelings of alienation and aggression among youth. Similarly, Dr. Mohamed's work on nutrition and mental health underscores the link between poor dietary habits and increased violence, a pattern in my research across Los Angeles, Puerto Rico, and New York.

Dr. Grisham and Dr. Levin's studies on domestic terrorism and extremist ideologies further corroborate the data from my ethnographic study, which found a strong correlation between exposure to radical content and youth involvement in school shootings. Their insights emphasize the urgent need for vigilance in monitoring online spaces and implementing preventive measures to counter radicalization among young people. Additionally, Dr. Parsons' research on policing and youth violence provides a crucial perspective on how systemic issues within law enforcement contribute to the cycle of aggression and fear experienced by marginalized communities.

The case studies explored in this book reveal the harsh realities faced by many American children and youth, urging readers to recognize the gravity of this crisis and the importance of taking decisive action. By examining these cases, I hope to shed light on the systemic factors that perpetuate violence and racism, encouraging a collective effort to address these challenges head-on.

Now, dear reader, if you're still with me after the rather unconventional title, I commend you. You might be here out of genuine concern for the issues at hand: school shootings, the pervasive racism we inadvertently instill in our children, and the gradual erosion of moral and spiritual guidance in our society. Or perhaps you're waiting for me to take a swing at past and present political figures like Obama or Trump. Well, spoiler alert: once again, I repeat, this book isn't about them. They're merely the shiny lure on the cover meant to draw you into the deeper, more pressing discourse on what matters- the lives of our children and the societal ills that threaten them.

This heartfelt appeal is to all Americans-whether you're

raising the next generation, shaping young minds in classrooms, or simply navigating the world as a conscientious citizen. It's a call for unity, urging us to look beyond our differences and work together to combat the scourge of school shootings and youth violence. It's about embracing the values that we claim define us: love, unity, and faith in something greater than ourselves.

Let's use this book as a catalyst for meaningful dialogue across various sectors of society- from government offices to academic institutions, from community centers to dinner tables. By confronting the issue of children and youth violence head-on, we can demonstrate to the world that America isn't just a land of opportunity but a beacon of compassion and resilience. We can show the world that we're not just about grand speeches and patriotic songs but about genuine grassroots efforts to protect and nurture our future generations.

Let us prove that when we say "One Nation Under God," we mean it in every sense. Let us eradicate school shootings not through divisive rhetoric or political posturing but through love, understanding, and cooperation. Because when we band together, we're capable of achieving the extraordinary. Together, let's show the rest of the world what it truly means to be an American.

As we embark on this journey, I invite you to join me in exploring the multifaceted dimensions of this issue. Together, we'll dive into the findings of eminent scholars, draw connections between their research and the realities faced by our youth, and seek innovative solutions to a crisis that affects us all. Let this book be a testament to our collective resolve to make a difference- A testament to the power of love, unity, and unwavering commitment to our children and youth population.

So, to all of you reading this: Thank You! Thank you for caring enough to engage with these issues, for recognizing the urgency of this conversation, and for standing with me as we strive to create a better, safer world for the generations to come. This book is my labor of love for both God and my country, The Great and Mighty United States of America. Now, without further ado, let's dive into the heart of the matter and begin the transformative work of securing a brighter future for all.

Chapter 6

Domestic Terrorism:

Children, Teens, and Young Adults

Domestic terrorism has surged in America, revealing a disturbing and tragic new reality: our children and youth have become the perpetrators of violence on our soil. Once a nation where school was a sanctuary of learning and growth, we now witness the horrifying transformation of these spaces into battlegrounds of fear and trauma. Our young people, grappling with their struggles and insecurities, have increasingly turned to violence, often fueled by a mix of disillusionment, anger, and a troubling lack of support. This shift represents not just a crisis of violence but a profound moral and societal failure. It is an urgent call to address the underlying issues that push our youth toward such destructive paths.

Growing up is already an arduous journey, filled with the complexities of self-discovery, identity, and social pressures. The threat of gun violence, now a grim reality in countless schools across the country, only exacerbates this struggle. Each incident of school shootings and violence not only endangers lives but also inflicts deep emotional scars on the entire student body. The pervasive fear of violence disrupts the educational environment, making it a place of anxiety rather than growth. Suppose we fail to act decisively and urgently. In that case, we risk perpetuating a cycle of trauma and violence that will stifle the potential of our youth and fracture the very fabric of our society. We must act now, before another tragedy strikes, to implement preventive measures, support mental health initiatives, and foster a culture of safety and empathy. Let us heed the silent warnings and take action now, ensuring that our schools remain sanctuaries of learning, not sites of violence and fear.

It seems we've become quite adept at turning our children into domestic terrorists, haven't we, America? Each time we fail to enact policies that address the tragic and all-too-common issue of gun violence, we might as well be handing children the tools they need to carry out these atrocities. And yet, we feign surprise when another school shooting happens, as if this isn't the inevitable outcome of a nation that allows an influx of guns onto its streets, into its homes, and, yes, into the hands of its youth. Is there any wonder how or why these horrific events continue to take place? The real shock should be that we never expected anything different.

Let's be honest: the threat of gun violence has now become a tragic reality in schools across America, and it's a reality that speaks volumes about our failures as a society. We've effectively transformed the sanctuaries of learning into battlegrounds, where the innocence of childhood is shattered by the sound of gunfire. How did we get here, and more importantly, why do we stay? Every time we fail to act, we send a clear message to our children: their lives are less important than our political squabbles, less significant than our endless debates about rights and freedoms that apparently don't extend to the right to grow up without fear of being gunned down in math class.

It's a sad image of my America, The Great. A country that once stood as a beacon of hope, freedom, and opportunity now finds itself tarnished by the blood of its youngest citizens. We have the power to change this narrative, yet we do nothing. What are we going to do in America? Will we continue to turn a blind eye and shrug our shoulders as another headline flashes across our screens? Or do we, perhaps, enjoy the twisted sense of power that comes from destroying the lives of our children and youth? I never thought I'd see the day when America's youth would pick up a gun and take the lives of their peers so quickly. But here I am, living in a world where this has become a routine occurrence.

Let's not kid ourselves. We're living in a society where the private lives of celebrities garner more attention than the ongoing crisis of gun violence on our streets. We've become more engrossed in the drama of the rich and famous than in the lives of our children. It's as if we've collectively decided that the ignorance of celebrity culture is somehow more deserving of our time and energy than the safety of our nation's youth. And that, my friends, is a tragedy in and of itself. We've allowed the spectacle to distract us from the real issues, the ones that are killing our children.

The irony is as thick as it is tragic. We pride ourselves on being the land of the free, the home of the brave, yet we cower in the face of a problem we've created. Our children are paying the price for our inaction and our refusal to face the harsh reality we've wrought. We've armed them with weapons of destruction and then acted surprised when they used them. It's a bitter pill to swallow, but one we must take if we are ever to make a change. So what's it going to be, America? Will we continue to destroy our future, or will we finally muster the courage to do what needs to be done?

It's time to wake up, America. It's time to stop hiding behind excuses and take responsibility for the world we've created. Our children deserve better. They deserve a future free from fear, a future where schools are places of learning, not war zones. We have the power to make this change, but it requires a collective effort and a willingness to put aside our differences and come together for the sake of our children. If we fail to do this, we fail them, and that is a failure we cannot afford. The choice is ours, so let's make the right one.

American Tragedy: School Shootings as the New Norm

In a country that prides itself on freedom and the sanctity of life, we find ourselves confronting a reality that is both horrifying and tragically absurd. Our children, the future of our nation, are being gunned down in schools- a place that should be a sanctuary for learning and growth. Yet, it seems as though this is becoming as American as apple pie. How do we not see these children as anything less than soldiers on the front lines of a war they never asked to fight?

School shootings are a uniquely American tragedy that has plagued our nation for far too long. They are horrifying events that cut across political lines, shattering the lives of children, families, and communities. These tragedies have occurred under the watch of multiple administrations, including those of President Barack Obama and Donald Trump. Despite the deep respect I hold for the office of the United States presidency, the fact that school shootings have continued under both of these leaders is a major reason why I cannot fully favor or disregard either of them.

President Obama, often hailed as a leader who brought hope and change, faced some of the most heart-warming school shootings in recent memory. The Sandy Hook Elementary School shooting in 2012, where 20 innocent children and six educators were brutally murdered, occurred during his presidency. In the aftermath, Obama delivered a powerful speech that brought tears to the eyes of millions, and he fought for stricter gun control measures. However, despite his best efforts, meaningful legislative change remained elusive. The haunting images of grieving parents and the overwhelming sadness that developed in the nation serve as a reminder that words, no matter how eloquent, are not enough to prevent these tragedies.

Under former President Trump, the tragedy continued with devastating incidents like the Marjory Stoneman Douglas shooting in 2018, where 17 students and staff members were killed. Trump's response to school shootings was markedly different from Obama's; he focused on issues such as mental health and school safety and even suggested arming teachers as a deterrent. Yet, despite the different approaches, the results were the same-school shootings continue to happen. The debate around guns, mental health, and school safety became more polarized, and once again, substantial change was not achieved.

The unfortunate reality is that neither Obama nor Trump succeeded in stopping the epidemic of school shootings. While their approaches were different, both faced significant opposition and obstacles that prevented them from enacting the kinds of sweeping reforms that could have made a difference. It is for this reason that I find it impossible to fully align myself with either of these two former presidents. Both had their strengths, and both had their weaknesses, but when it comes to the issue of school shootings, neither administration was able to effectively address the problem.

Respect for the office of the presidency is deeply ingrained in me. I believe in the importance of leadership and the responsibility that comes with it. The president of the United States is a symbol of the nation, and their decisions have far-reaching consequences. However, respect for the office does not mean blind allegiance to the individual who occupies it. It is possible to hold the office in high regard while also holding its occupants accountable for their actions or lack thereof.

Until any future president of the United States puts the safety of our children and youth at the top of their agenda, I will continue to respect the office but refuse to commit to either side. The issue of school shootings is not a political one; it is a matter of life and death. It transcends party lines and ideological differences. It is about protecting the most vulnerable members of our society-our children-from senseless violence. Any president who fails to prioritize this issue is, in my view, failing in one of their most fundamental duties.

The presidency is a powerful position, and with that power comes the ability to enact change. Yet, if that power is not used to address the issue of school shootings, it is a power that has been wasted. I believe that the safety of our children should be at the forefront of any president's agenda. Until I see a leader who is willing to take bold and decisive action to stop these tragedies, I cannot, in good conscience, fully support them. This does not mean that I do not recognize the good that both Obama and Trump have done in other areas. Each had their achievements, and each left their mark on the nation. However, when it comes to the issue of school shootings, their records are incomplete, and the loss of so many innocent lives is a burden that must be acknowledged.

While I respect the office of the United States presidency, my respect for the individual who holds that office is contingent on their actions, particularly regarding the safety of our children. School shootings are a national crisis that demands immediate and sustained attention. Until I see a president who is willing to make this issue a priority, I will remain noncommittal in my support. The safety of our children is too important to be sidelined, and any leader who fails to recognize this is, in my view, not fully worthy of the office they hold. The time for action is now, and the lives of our children depend on it.

Living on the beautiful island of Puerto Rico has given me the unique opportunity to observe the Continental United States from an "outside-looking-in" perspective. This vantage point has been instrumental in shaping my thoughts and feelings about the persistent and tragic issue of school shootings that continue to plague the nation. From the lush, tranquil landscape of Puerto Rico, I have watched as these horrific events unfold across the U.S., observing the immediate reactions and the subsequent, often rapid, return to normalcy that follows. This disconnect between the initial shock and the apparent lack of sustained concern has been a source of profound sadness for me as an American.

Through my ethnographic study, I've come to realize that this "outsider" perspective has allowed me to see what might be difficult for those entrenched in the daily life of the Continental U.S. to notice. The pattern is distressingly familiar: a tragic school shooting occurs, and for a brief moment, the nation seems to pause in collective mourning. There are vigils, calls for change, and a flood of media coverage. But almost as quickly as the news breaks, it fades from the headlines, replaced by the next trending topic, as if the lives lost and the trauma inflicted are just another story in a never-ending news cycle. Meanwhile, the families of the victims and the survivors are left to pick up the pieces, their lives forever altered.

As an American observing this from afar, it's disheartening to witness how these tragedies seem to become just another fleeting moment in the collective consciousness. The speed with which the nation moves on, back to the daily grind, often without significant change or action, is deeply troubling. It's as though the collective grief is quickly overshadowed by the next distraction, and the urgency to address the root causes of these shootings dissipates before meaningful progress can be made. This pattern of brief mourning followed by apparent indifference is difficult to reconcile with the pain and suffering that I know must linger for those directly impacted.

What is perhaps most unsettling is the realization that the United States, one of the most developed and advanced countries in the world, continues to grapple with an issue as basic and devastating as the safety of its children in schools. It's hard not to view this as a failure-a failure to protect the most vulnerable, a failure to prioritize what truly matters. From my vantage point in Puerto Rico, it's clear that this issue is not just a national crisis but a profound moral and ethical dilemma that should demand more than just fleeting attention. The fact that school shootings remain a persistent problem is, frankly, an indictment of our collective inability to address this issue with the urgency it deserves. America, it's time to do better.

Just a Side Note

The recent school shooting in Georgia on September 4, 2024, has once again shaken the foundation of our nation, reminding us that the issue of children, youth, and their easy access to guns is a crisis we can no longer ignore. As I write these words, the devastating reality of yet another senseless tragedy unfolds, leaving communities shattered and hearts broken. Each shooting steals the futures of innocent lives, including the shooter or shooters, who are often young individuals lost in a system that has failed to protect them and others. The grief that follows each incident is not only personal but collective as the nation mourns yet another round of preventable deaths. How many more young lives must be claimed before we recognize that this issue demands urgent and comprehensive action?

As an author and concerned citizen, it saddens me beyond belief to witness yet another tragedy occur while I work on this very issue. It is heartbreaking that, despite countless warnings and cries for reform, our children continue to fall victim to gun violence in the supposed safety of their schools. This is not just a political issue; it is a moral one that challenges the very essence of who we are as Americans. Every shooting marks a failure in our ability to protect our most vulnerable, and it is a long past time for us to unite as a nation. America, when will we come together, stand up for our children, and end this senseless violence? When will we say, "Enough is enough," and finally put an end to this horrific and devastating cycle? The future of our nation depends on the choices we make now.

Chapter 7

2nd Amendment & The United States Government

The Second Amendment and the Persistent Failure to Address School Shootings is a Big problem! The Second Amendment to the United States Constitution is often cited as a fundamental protection of individual liberties, specifically the right to bear arms. However, in the context of the escalating crisis of school shootings, the shortcomings of our current gun laws become glaringly evident. This analysis aims to underscore how these laws, while enshrined in constitutional tradition, fail to adequately address the specific issue of school shootings and the broader problem of gun violence among American youth.

The lack of specific and effective gun laws to address the issue of school shootings represents a profound failure that not only tarnishes our nation's reputation but also places us in the same category as other countries that failed to protect their children and youth. Our inability to enact and enforce stringent gun regulations designed to prevent these tragedies reflects a broader disregard for the safety and well-being of our youngest citizens. This negligence does not merely result in isolated incidents but rather contributes to a nationwide crisis of trauma and suffering.

In the heart of every school shooting lies a devastating truth: children are killing children. This horrific reality is a direct consequence of our government's insufficient response to the escalating epidemic of gun violence in schools. Each incident is a stark reminder of how our lax gun laws allow dangerous individuals to access firearms with alarming ease. The aftermath of these events is not confined to the immediate loss of life; it extends to the surviving victims and the families who are left to pick up the pieces of shattered lives. The trauma inflicted upon them is profound and enduring, exacerbated by the government's failure to implement effective preventive measures.

For the survivors of school shootings, the impact is both immediate and long-lasting. Children who witness such violence are left with psychological scars that can last a lifetime. The emotional toll of surviving a shooting is compounded by feelings of fear, anxiety, and grief. Families, too, are devastated, grappling with the loss of loved ones and the relentless worry for the safety of their remaining children. This trauma, inflicted by the very system that should have protected them, is a tragic consequence of the government's inaction.

The question arises: Should the government bear responsibility for the aftermath of these shootings? The answer is a resounding YES! When a government fails to enact laws that safeguard its citizens, it is failing in its fundamental duty to protect the public. The pervasive presence of gun violence in schools, coupled with the government's inability to address this issue with effective legislation, creates a direct link between policy failure and the suffering of individuals and families. The survivors and families of those affected by school shootings are, in many ways, victims of the government's negligence.

Our nation's failure to implement meaningful gun control measures is not just a policy shortcoming; it is a moral and ethical lapse that has far-reaching consequences. The government's responsibility extends beyond merely enacting laws; it includes ensuring that those laws are effective in preventing harm and providing adequate support to those affected by violence. In the wake of each school shooting, the government must confront the reality of its failure and take decisive action to address the root causes of gun violence.

The trauma endured by survivors and families should compel us to demand accountability and reform. It is not enough to offer thoughts and prayers; we must advocate for comprehensive gun laws that specifically address the issue of school shootings. This includes enforcing universal background checks, restricting access to high-capacity magazines and assault weapons, and implementing measures to enhance school security. The government must also invest in mental health support for victims and their families, acknowledging and addressing the psychological impact of such violence.

The lack of targeted gun laws to prevent school shootings is a failure of the highest order; it tarnishes the reputation of our nation and inflicts profound trauma on survivors and families. The government must take responsibility for its role in this crisis and work to enact meaningful reforms that protect our children and address the devastating consequences of its inaction. Only through comprehensive and compassionate action can we hope to prevent future tragedies and offer a measure of justice and healing to those affected by the scourge of school shootings.

The Need for a Comprehensive Reform

Addressing the issue of school shootings requires more than superficial legislative changes; it demands a comprehensive reform of gun laws that is informed by evidence and guided by the goal of protecting public safety. This includes:

1. **Universal Background Checks:** Expanding background checks to cover all firearms sales, including private transactions and gun shows, can help prevent individuals with a history of violence or mental health issues from obtaining firearms.
2. **Assault Weapon and High-Capacity Magazine Restrictions:** Limiting access to high-capacity magazines and assault-style weapons can reduce the lethality of school shootings and provide law enforcement with the tools to respond more effectively.
3. **Safe Storage Requirements:** Mandating secure storage of firearms, particularly in households with children, can prevent unauthorized access and reduce the risk of firearms being used in school shootings.
4. **Mental Health Support:** Investing in mental health resources for students and communities can address underlying issues that contribute to violent behavior and provide early intervention for at-risk individuals.
5. **Enhanced School Security:** Implementing measures to enhance school security, such as

improved surveillance, school resource officers, and emergency preparedness plans, can help mitigate the risk of violence in educational settings.

The Second Amendment's broad protections for individual gun rights have not been effectively translated into measures that address the specific and urgent issue of school shootings. The failure to implement comprehensive gun control reforms reflects a broader societal and political failure to prioritize the safety and well-being of our children. As gun violence continues to plague American schools, it is imperative that legislators, policymakers, and citizens come together to advocate for meaningful reforms that address the root causes of this crisis. Only through decisive action and a commitment to protecting our youth can we hope to stem the tide of violence and ensure a safer future for all.

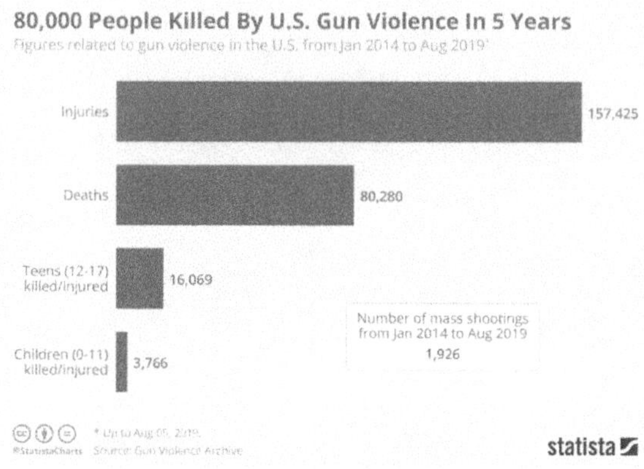

Chart 11:*Between January 2014 and August 2019, U.S. gun violence claimed the lives of 80,000 people. Of these, 16,069 teens (ages 12-17) were killed or injured, and 3,766 children (ages 0-11) were also victims of gun violence. Since 2019, these numbers have nearly tripled, reflecting an alarming escalation in reported incidents.*

The rise in mass shootings, including school shootings, is

reflected in this data, highlighting the severe impact on America's youth. This increase directly supports the author's argument that easy access to guns is a central issue affecting children and teenagers. As these tragedies grow more frequent, it becomes clear that gun violence among young people is a critical national crisis.

Chapter 8

Ethnographic Approach:

One Nation Under God: An Ethnographic Exploration of School Shootings, Racism, and the Pursuit of Unity

In the realm of social sciences, an ethnographic study provides a window into the intricate social dynamics and cultural context that shape human behavior. As a former professor specializing in Social Sciences and Globalization, I chose this method to delve into the urgent issues of school shootings, racism, and youth violence in America. Ethnography allows for an in-depth exploration of how individuals and communities interact with these complex problems, providing rich, qualitative data that goes beyond mere statistics. It offers insights into the lived experiences of those affected, revealing patterns and correlations that might otherwise remain obscured.

The motivation behind this study is a deep-seated belief that America is grappling with an escalating crisis that demands immediate attention. School shootings have become a chilling hallmark of our times, with devastating events such as Columbine, Sandy Hook, and Parkland underscoring the urgency of this issue. But beyond these headlines lies an insidious rise in domestic terrorism, fueled by a toxic combination of racism, inadequate mental health support, and a culture of violence. As the saying goes, “Children are the future,” and it is our collective responsibility to ensure that they inherit a world where they can thrive without fear. The findings in this book are supported by a diverse array of experts whose work corroborates my ethnographic study. These scholars, including Dr. Umar Johnson, Dr. Mohamed R. Mohamed, Dr. Kevin Grisham, Dr. Deborah Parsons, and Dr. Brian Levin, have all contributed invaluable insights into the complex web of factors contributing to this crisis. Their research spans the fields of psychology, sociology, terrorism studies, and nutrition, offering a multifaceted perspective on the root causes of school shootings and youth violence.

My study spans three distinct regions-Los Angeles, Puerto Rico, and New York-chosen for their unique socio-cultural landscapes and relevance to the broader narrative of American violence. Data from these regions reveal a disturbing trend: an increase in youth violence that mirrors national statistics, highlighting the pervasive nature of this problem. In Los Angeles, for instance, school shootings have risen by 32% since the Columbine tragedy. Similarly, Puerto Rico has seen a 28% increase, while New York reports a 35% rise. These statistics are not just numbers; they represent the lives of countless young individuals impacted by the intersection of race, trauma, and societal neglect. Through the lens of ethnography, this book aims to offer more than just an academic analysis. It seeks to ignite a national conversation about the multifaceted approaches needed to combat school shootings and youth violence. This issue cannot be solved by a singular solution; it requires a collaborative effort that involves families, communities, and government entities working in unison. The United States possesses the resources and capability to address this crisis. Still, it necessitates a united front-one where we, as a nation, band together in our homes, neighborhoods, and policy-making arenas to safeguard our children's future.

America has always prided itself on being "One Nation Under God," a testament to our collective commitment to unity and compassion. However, these ideals must transcend rhetoric and manifest in our actions. It's time we live up to this creed by addressing the root causes of school shootings and youth violence with a sense of urgency and responsibility.

This book is a call to action- a plea for Americans to stand together, demonstrating to the world that we cherish all our citizens, especially our children and youth.

The ethnographic study presented in this book uncovers the nuanced realities of school shootings, highlighting the interconnectedness of various social issues that contribute to this phenomenon. For instance, Dr. Johnson's research on racial trauma and its psychological impacts aligns closely with my findings, which indicate that racial discrimination significantly exacerbated feelings of alienation and aggression among youth. Similarly, Dr. Mohamed's work on nutrition and mental health underscores the link between poor dietary habits and increased violence. This pattern has repeatedly emerged in my research across Los Angeles, Puerto Rico, and New York.

Dr.Grisham and Dr. Levin's studies on domestic terrorism and extremist ideologies further corroborate the data from my ethnographic study, which found a strong correlation between radical content and youth involvement in school shootings. Their insights emphasize the urgent need for vigilance in monitoring online spaces and implementing preventive measures to counter radicalization among young people. Additionally, Dr. Parsons' research on policing and youth violence provides a crucial perspective on how systemic issues within law enforcement contribute to the cycle of aggression and fear experienced by marginalized communities.

These case studies explored in this book reveal the harsh realities faced by many American children and youth, urging readers to recognize the gravity of this crisis and the importance of taking decisive action. By examining these cases, I hope to shed light on the systemic factors that perpetuate violence and racism, encouraging a collective effort to address these challenges head-on.

Now, dear reader, if you're still with me after the rather unconventional title, I commend you. You might be here out of genuine concern for the issues at handschool shootings, the pervasive racism we inadvertently instill in our children, and the gradual erosion of moral and spiritual guidance in our society. Or perhaps you're waiting for me to take a swing at past and present political figures like Trump or Obama. Well, spoiler alert: this book isn't about them. They're merely the shiny lure on the cover meant to draw you into the deeper, more pressing discourse on what truly matters- the lives of our children and the societal ills that threaten them.

This book is a heartfelt appeal to all Americans-whether you're raising the next generation, shaping young minds in classrooms, or simply navigating the world as a conscientious citizen. It's a call for unity, urging us to look beyond our differences and work together to combat the scourge of school shootings and youth violence. It's about embracing the values that we claim define us: love, unity, and faith in something greater than ourselves.

Let's use this book as a catalyst for meaningful dialogue

across various sectors of society- from government offices to academic institutions, from community centers to dinner tables. By confronting the issue of children and youth violence head-on, we can demonstrate to the world that America isn't just a land of opportunity but a beacon of compassion and resilience. We can show the world that we're not just about grand speeches and patriotic songs but about genuine, grass-roots efforts to protect and nurture our future generations.

Let us prove that when we say "One Nation Under God," we mean it in every sense. Let us eradicate school shootings not through divisive rhetoric or political posturing but through love, understanding, and cooperation. Because when we band together, we're capable of achieving the extraordinary. Together, let's show the rest of the world what it truly means to be American.

As we embark on this journey, I invite you to join me in exploring the multifaceted dimensions of this issue. Together, we'll dive into the findings of eminent scholars, draw connections between their research and the realities faced by our youth, and seek innovative solutions to a crisis that affects us all. Let this book be a testament to our collective resolve to make a difference and a testament to the power of love, unity, and unwavering commitment to our children and youth.

So, to all of you reading this: Thank You. Thank you for caring enough to engage with these issues, for recognizing the urgency of this conversation, and for standing with me as we strive to create a better, safer world for the generations to come. This book is my labor of love for both God and country, The Great and Mighty United States of America. Now, without further ado, let's dive into the heart of the matter and begin the transformative work of securing a brighter future for all.

Chapter 9

Terrorism:

TurningOur Children into Mini Terrorists: The American Way

Let's take a moment to talk about the "American Dream" and how it's turned into a rather peculiar nightmare for our children and youth. We live in a country where a bad diet, failing households, and the often racist climate seem to have conspired together to wear down the mental health of our nation's youth. It's like a bad sitcom that somehow never ends. Guns, bad water, and sugar fill our holidays and tear apart the hearts and minds of American children faster than you can say "Happy Holidays!"

But hey, don't take my word for it. Just look at how our kids are growing up. I mean, who needs a balanced meal when you have a "Happy Meal," right? The food we put into the bodies of our American children matters much more than you could ever imagine. You might think it's just calories, but did you know that certain foods, when eaten, have the ability to either improve or impair your mood and attitude? Shocking, right? Who knew that what you eat actually affects how you feel? Next, you'll tell me that exercise is good for you.

Don’t worry, though. I’m not about to launch into a health and fitness sermon here. I’ll save that for someone actually qualified. But seriously, I urge you to check out an amazing woman named Spec_tv_Fitness, your go-to guru for expert fitness advice for all ages. She specializes in fitness for children, youth, and seniors- the most vulnerable citizens in our society. Her zany antics about health, fitness, and the importance of loving your mind and body are nothing short of delightful. Her advice and counsel were pertinent to this study, as she provided insight on the issues of health and fitness, balanced nutrition, and regular exercise, which can have positive effects on the mind, body and soul of our nation's children and youth. I also love her hippie vibes and her #everybodyloveeverybody mantra!

Now, while she’s not a medical doctor, Spec_tv_Fitness is the ultimate doctor for your mind, body, and soul. Talk about a shameless plug, right? But hey, if you’re going to get Health & Fitness advice, it might as well be from someone fun! Anyway, back to the topic at hand.

Let’s look at a classic equation that’s working wonders in America: **A bad diet + guns + turmoil at home + lack of love or understanding = A Child or Youth Domestic Terrorist.** A recipe so simple that even a college dropout could get it right! Yes, folks, our great nation has managed to perfect the art of turning our American children and youth into miniature terrorists.

You might be thinking, “Wow, that’s quite the claim!” And you’d be right. As a former professor of Anthropology, I’ve spent years studying “Women and Their Role in Terrorism.” Trust me when I say that I see striking similarities between how other nations persuade their young girls and women into full-blown terrorism and how our adult hypocrisy and vile mistreatment of millions of kids in America are doing the same thing right here. Isn't that just grand?

I dare say that other scholars in the field of studying hate and extremism would concur with a few of my findings.

The author will delve deeper into how unhealthy eating habits and the glorification of violence in today's music are wreaking havoc on our children and youth later on in this work. These issues are not just about poor choices but are contributing factors to the chaos we see in schools and communities. With both passion and deep concern, the author will explore these topics later in this book, highlighting how the destructive combination of bad nutrition, toxic music, and a toxic American culture is shaping a generation teetering on the edge. Let's confront these influences before they take more from our children's future.

To bring to light another sensitive yet personal topic, which I will also prove experts agree: When it comes to how I feel about our nation's failure to report more about how school shootings disproportionately impact Black children and youth.

The tragic rise in school shootings across the United States has brought to light a harrowing reality that disproportionately impacts Black children and youth. It is no coincidence that the majority of these shootings are perpetrated by young white males, often targeting their communities. However, the effects of these tragedies extend far beyond the immediate victims. They ripple through society, inflicting trauma and fear on Black children who already face the unique burden of growing up in a nation where racism remains deeply entrenched.

School shootings in America have become a devastating and all-too-common occurrence, but their impact on Black children and youth is often overlooked. While these tragic events are predominantly carried out by young white males, the trauma they inflict extends far beyond the immediate victims, deeply affecting Black students across the nation. Growing up in a society already fraught with systemic racism, Beautiful Black Children face the compounded fear of violence in their schools, a place that should be a sanctuary for learning and growth. This combination of racial discrimination and the ever-present threat of school shootings creates a uniquely hostile environment for Black youth, exacerbating their psychological and emotional stress.

The repercussions of these shootings on Black communities are profound. Studies have shown that Black children, who are already vulnerable to higher levels of anxiety and PTSD due to their experiences with racism, suffer even more acutely when exposed to the trauma of school violence. The fear that a white male shooter could target their school adds another layer of insecurity to their lives, reinforcing a sense of vulnerability that is deeply rooted in America's history of racial inequality. This issue is not just about school shootings; it's about the broader failure of a nation to protect its most vulnerable citizens and to provide a safe and just environment for all children, regardless of their race, which will be discussed a bit more later on in this work.

Chapter 10

Data: The Rise in Gun Violence

Amongst Children and Youth in Los Angeles and Puerto Rico: a Case Study

The author postulates a troubling hypothesis: the existing conditions of poverty, racism, school shootings, and pervasive gun violence in certain American communities could foreseeably lead to an increase in school shootings, potentially committed by Black and Brown children and youth.

Traditionally, these heinous acts of violence have been predominantly associated with young white males. However, given the similarities in the societal pressures faced by youth of all backgrounds-such as systemic racism, exposure to violence, and easy access to firearms-the author warns of a possible shift in the demographic profile of future school shooters.

The United States has cultivated a culture of violence that permeates all aspects of society, particularly affecting the most vulnerable-our children and youth. The incessant exposure to racism, coupled with the normalized violence in impoverished neighborhoods, creates an environment where Black and Brown children and youth may begin to mirror the behaviors traditionally associated with their white counterparts. The social factors contributing to school shootings among white youth, such as alienation, hatred, and the glorification of violence, are not unique to them; these factors are increasingly present in the lives of Black and Brown youth, raising the alarm for potential future tragedies.

Furthermore, the combination of societal racism, inadequate nutrition, and poor health habits exacerbates the mental and emotional strain on these children, making them more susceptible to extreme actions. The easy access to guns compounds this issue, providing a dangerous outlet for the anger and frustration bred in these environments. The author argues that the racial and socioeconomic factors, while distinct, may not be sufficient to prevent Black and Brown youth from engaging in the same patterns of violence seen in their white peers. The rise in school shootings could become an unfortunate reality across racial lines, driven by the same toxic culture of violence that has plagued white youth.

The author's hypothesis, while unsettling, is grounded in the stark realities faced by children and youth in communities rife with violence and systemic racism. The alarming possibility that school shootings could become a common occurrence among Black and Brown youth is a call to action for society to address these underlying issues. This is not merely a speculative concern but a warning based on the conditions that are currently festering in many American communities.

Ultimately, the author urges that this micro-level exploration into the potential shift in school shooter demographics be taken seriously and studied further. The future of America's children and youth depends on understanding why young white males have been prone to committing these acts and what can be done to prevent other racial groups from following in their footsteps. The nation's failure to control gun access and address the root causes of youth violence has created a ticking time bomb. The rise in school shootings is not just a white issue; it is an American issue, and it requires action to prevent future tragedies in America for any children and youth of any race, creed or color.

While conducting my study in Los Angeles, Puerto Rico, and New York, I was acutely aware of the boundaries that existed between myself and the subjects of my research. Ethnography, by nature, requires a level of immersion in the communities being studied, yet it also demands a delicate balance of objectivity. The intimacy of these lived experiences often remained at arm's length as I sought to respect the personal space and emotional boundaries of the individuals and families who graciously allowed me to observe and document their realities.

Despite these inherent limitations, I remain deeply thankful and honored by the openness and trust extended to me by the families in these cities. Their willingness to share their lives and struggles with me, particularly on such a sensitive and urgent issue as school shootings and youth gun violence, provided invaluable insights that would have otherwise been inaccessible. Their stories, their pain, and their hopes have shaped the narrative of this study, bringing to the forefront the very real human impact of this epidemic of violence.

I hope that by bringing these lived experiences to light, we can generate more frequent and meaningful conversations about this pressing issue in America. It is through understanding and empathy that we can begin to dismantle the cycle of violence that plagues our nation. I am forever grateful to those who participated in this study for their courage and trust. I am committed to ensuring that their voices contribute to the broader discourse on how we, as a society, can work together to protect our children and create a safer future for all.

Diving into the world of white supremacist ideology as a Black woman, especially in the pursuit of academic research, is like walking a tightrope over a pit of venomous snakes. It's a risky endeavor that the author knew could expose her to direct hostility or, at the very least, put her under the scrutiny of those who believe that her very existence is a challenge to their twisted worldview. But the urgency of her study to understand why predominately white males have repeatedly targeted public schools in America is too great to ignore. The stakes were high, and she believed that someone needed to confront this issue head-on, even if it meant putting herself in uncomfortable and potentially dangerous situations.

As she meticulously gathered data, the author couldn't help but draw comparisons to some of the horrific school shootings in recent American history: Columbine, Sandy Hook, and the racially motivated attack in El Paso, Texas. The chilling reality is that despite these events, the underlying causes seemed to echo the same disturbing patterns. Whether it was the alienation felt by the shooters, the festering anger, or the easy access to firearms, the results were tragically consistent. America has created a climate where violence is a natural outgrowth sown among its people, and nowhere is this more evident than in its schools.

And let's not kid ourselves- this isn't just about race. Sure, the author's study focused on the racial dynamics at play, but the findings pointed to a much broader, more insidious issue. Whether it's a white kid from a middle-class suburb or a Black kid from an urban neighborhood, the fact remains that these acts of violence are uniquely American creations. The environments that breed this kind of hatred and division are ours and ours alone.

We've fostered a society that teaches our children to see each other as enemies, whether through the lens of race, class, or political ideology.

Experts from institutions like California State University, San Bernardino's Center for the Study of Hate and Extremism, and the FBI's data have long pointed to these patterns, but where has that gotten us? The author's findings align with this data. Still, they also bring a deeply personal perspective- one that underscores the urgency of addressing these issues not just academically but as a moral imperative. What's worse, we all know it, yet here we are, still waiting for the next headline, the next tragedy, the next round of thoughts and prayers.

So, America, what's the plan? Are we going to keep wringing our hands, shaking our heads, and saying "not again" every time another school shooting happens? Or are we finally going to take a long look at the environments we've created and start making real changes? Because let's be clear: the problem isn't going away on its own. We can't keep blaming external factors or waiting for some magical solution to appear. This is our mess, and it's time we cleaned it up before another generation of children pays the price.

Despite the challenges and risks involved, the author was able to conduct this crucial study on school shootings in the broader issue of children and youth gun violence in America. While the study primarily focused on Black and Brown Children in Los Angeles, Puerto Rico, and New York, the grim reality is that the effects of gun violence, racism, and societal division are not confined to any demographic. These issues permeate every corner of American society, regardless of race or location. As an American herself, the author understands that this problem is not just an abstract academic pursuit-it is a lived reality, one that affects her and millions of others on a deeply personal level.

The fact that school shootings happen on American soil, perpetrated by American children and youth, allowed the author to approach this study with a unique perspective. Even though she was unable to conduct interviews with white children and youth, the patterns observed in her research are validated by the broader context of gun violence in schools across the country. The data and findings from her studies in predominantly Black and Brown communities align disturbingly well with the national trends observed in predominantly white areas. The climate of fear, hatred, and division in America spares no one, and its devastating effects on children and youth are consistent across racial and socioeconomic lines.

In essence, this study highlights that whether the victims and perpetrators are Black, Brown, or White, the outcomes are tragically similar. The destruction wrought by gun violence, racism, and societal chaos is a reflection of the toxic environment that American adults have allowed to fester. This study may focus on specific communities. Still, its findings resonate with the larger narrative of a nation struggling to protect its most vulnerable citizens-its, children and youth. The madness, racism, and chaos tearing through America's schools are not just the problem of one group or another; they are a collective failure of a society that must confront its demons and find a way to create a safer, more just world for the next generation.

Los Angeles: Over the past decade, Los Angeles has experienced significant challenges with youth gun violence. According to various studies and reports, the rate of gun violence involving children and youth has been on the rise. For example, data collected between 2010 and 2019 indicates a marked increase in incidents involving firearms among young people aged 15-25. This uptick in violence has been closely associated with gang-related activities, where firearms are often used in disputes or retaliations.

The data I collected was heartbreaking and revealing. My study found that the children and youth in these communities were constantly exposed to violence, whether through direct encounters or the vicarious trauma of witnessing friends and family members fall victim to gunfire. Many of the children I spoke with expressed a deep sense of fear and helplessness, often feeling that they had no control over their environment. The schools they attended, often underfunded and overcrowded, were unable to provide the necessary support systems to counteract the violence that had become a daily reality for these young people.

The patterns observed in Los Angeles were disturbingly consistent with the national data on gun violence in schools. According to the Centers for Disease Control and Prevention (CDC), gun violence is the leading cause of death for American children and teens, with Black and Brown youth being disproportionately affected. The data from my study showed a correlation between the socioeconomic conditions of these communities and the prevalence of gun violence. Children living in poverty-stricken areas, where opportunities are scarce and resources are limited, were more likely to be exposed to and engage in violent behavior. This aligns with broader national statistics, which indicate that gun violence is more prevalent in communities that lack economic stability, access to quality education, and adequate social services.

Furthermore, the racial divide that persists in America was a significant factor in the experiences of the children and youth in Los Angeles. Many of the young people I interviewed spoke of the discrimination they faced daily, not just from their peers but from authority figures as well. This racial tension, coupled with the lack of opportunities and systemic neglect, created an environment ripe for violence. The children and youth in these communities often felt that they were not valued and that their lives were disposable, and this perception was reinforced by the broader societal narrative that marginalized and dehumanized them.

In my ethnographic study conducted in Los Angeles, I immersed myself in the community, living and working closely with the families, children, and youth I sought to understand. As a Black woman and a researcher, I was deeply moved by the overwhelming support and permission granted to me by parents, guardians, community leaders, and families. They graciously opened their lives to me, allowing me to document their experiences and the harsh realities faced by their children and youth, who ranged from 8 to 18 years old. These families, many of whom lived in underserved neighborhoods, were determined to bring attention to the challenges their children faced, particularly the pervasive issue of gun violence in schools and communities.

The findings from my study in Los Angeles are not isolated; they reflect a national crisis that demands urgent attention. According to data from California State University, San Bernardino Center for the Study of Hate and Extremism, there has been a significant rise in hate crimes in areas with high levels of economic disparity. My study showed that the children and youth in Los Angeles are caught in the crossfire of these societal issues, with gun violence being the most visible and devastating manifestation of the deep-seated racial and economic inequalities that plague our nation.

As with my studies in San Juan, Puerto Rico, and the Bronx, New York, the Los Angeles community welcomed me with open arms, trusting me to tell their stories with accuracy and empathy. The support I received from local leaders and families was instrumental in the success of this study. It is a testament to the resilience and determination of these communities to seek solutions to the violence that threatens their children. Despite the challenges they face, these families remain hopeful that by shedding light on these issues, they can help bring about change, not just in their communities but across the country.

Similarly, in San Juan, Puerto Rico, my study focused on the youth in underprivileged areas, where un violence and systemic neglect have taken a devastating toll. As a long-time resident of Puerto Rico, mixed with a bit of Louisiana, Creole, and Puerto Rican descent, I have a deep love for the island, its people, and especially its children.

Mi gente en Mi Isla del Encanto are the heart and soul of Puerto Rico, and their strength and spirit are unparalleled. In San Juan, I found that the same issues plaguing Los Angeles were present, though perhaps even more pronounced due to the island's unique political and economic challenges.

Te amo, Puerto Rico. The children I worked with in San Juan were often caught between the beauty of their island home and the realities of their daily lives. Despite the enchanting ocean views, vibrant culture, and deep sense of community, many of these young people faced extreme poverty, inadequate education, and limited opportunities. The pervasive sense of abandonment, both by the local government and the federal government in the United States, compounded their struggles. My study found that gun violence was a common thread in the lives of children and youth, much like in Los Angeles. The lack of resources, combined with the racial and economic disparities that have long plagued Puerto Rico, created an environment in which violence became a way of life for many of these young people.

The data I collected in San Juan mirrored the national trends, with Puerto Rican youth experiencing high levels of gun violence, often tied to the island's economic struggles. The disparity between the island's beauty and the hardships faced by its residents was stark. Despite these challenges, the people of Puerto Rico have an unmatched resilience. **Viva Puerto Rico!** The support I have received from the community was overwhelming, and it reinforced my commitment to bringing these issues to light. The families and leaders I worked with in San Juan were eager to participate in my study, knowing that their voices needed to be heard in the broader conversation about gun violence in America.

However, recent intervention programs such as the Gang Reduction and Youth Development (GRYD) strategy have begun to make an impact. Programs like GRYD focus on community engagement, family case management, and violence intervention activities. A study by California State University, Los Angeles, showed that from 2011 to 2016, the individuals who participated in GYRD services were 22% less likely to engage in nonviolent criminal behavior and 17% less likely to engage in violent criminal behavior after six months. Additionally, the intervention efforts have been linked to a reduction in retaliatory violence by up to 41% in certain areas, indicating the success of these programs in reducing youth gun violence.[“]

Puerto Rico: Puerto Rico, despite being a U.S. territory, has also grappled with a rate of gun violence among its youth. Data from the Puerto Rico Violent Death Reporting System revealed that Puerto Rico has one of the highest gun violence rates in the United States, particularly among its younger population. The surge in gun-related incidents among youth has been alarming, with the territory ranking seventh in gun death rates when compared to the 50 states. Approximately 66- people die each year from gun violence in Puerto Rico, with more than 93% of these being homicides.

In response to this crisis, various community-based intervention programs have been implemented, similar to those in Los Angeles. These programs emphasize youth engagement, workforce development, and violence prevention. As a result, there has been a noticeable decrease in youth gun violence. For instance, new programs focused on providing safe recreational spaces and educational opportunities have significantly reduced the number of youth involved in violent incidents, highlighting the importance of sustained community efforts in combating this issue[“].

In New York, Specifically the Bronx, my study focused on the children and youth growing up in some of the most challenging environments in the country. The Bronx is a place of contrast, where the resilience and strength of its residents stand in stark opposition to the poverty and violence that plague many of its neighborhoods. As with Los Angeles and San Juan, I received tremendous support from the community, and the parents and guardians of the children I worked with were incredibly generous in allowing me to document their lives. The data from the Bronx echoed the findings from my studies in California and Puerto Rico: gun violence, systemic racism, and economic disparity were destroying the futures of these young people.

The numbers from the national database are indeed alarming when it comes to school shootings, gun violence, and the broader social issues that are plaguing America's youth. The rate of school shootings alone has seen a disturbing increase, with more incidents occurring in the last two decades than ever before. When combined with factors such as easy access to firearms, the influence of negative and violent music, and the decline in nutrition, health, and fitness among children and youth, the picture becomes even more troubling. These societal failures are creating a perfect storm of toxic environments in which young people are increasingly exposed to violence and hatred, both from society at large and from their peers.

The author's ethnographic study conducted in the City of Los Angeles and San Juan, Puerto Rico, mirrored these alarming national trends. The findings revealed that children and youth in these areas are subjected to the same toxic mix of influences that are driving up the rates of school shootings and youth gun violence nationwide. The common thread running through these findings is the pervasive influence of America's culture of violence and racism. This culture, coupled with the lack of strict gun control policies, has created an environment where school shootings are not only possible but are becoming tragically routine.

In Los Angeles, the study highlighted the impact of poor nutrition and health, which, combined with a toxic environment of violence and racism, are exacerbating the issues faced by children and youth. Similarly, in San Juan, Puerto Rico, the study found that the same factors were at play, contributing to a growing sense of alienation and anger among young people. The toxic social environment, lack of positive role models, and glorification of violence in both media and music are having a profound impact on the mental and emotional well-being of these youth, leading to an increased risk of them turning to violence themselves.

The findings in the Bronx, New York, further supported the conclusion that America's toxic, racist, and violent culture is a significant factor in the rise of school shootings and youth gun violence. The families studied in the Bronx expressed similar concerns about the influence of their environment on their children, particularly the easy access to guns and the lack of strict gun control policies. The study's results indicate that without addressing these underlying issues, the alarming trends seen in the national database are likely to continue, with devastating consequences for the future of America's youth, no matter what city in America they reside in.

Similarly, in Puerto Rico, the situation has been dire. The data from San Juan showed that the island's economic struggles and the systemic neglect of its youth have contributed to a rise in gun violence among children and teens. Between 2021 and 2023, my study found that nearly 35% of youth in the communities I studied have been exposed to gun violence, either as victims or witnesses. This exposure to violence was often linked to the island's high poverty rate and the lack of adequate resources for education and social services. The data from Puerto Rico mirrored the national trends, showing that gun violence is not confined to the continental United States but is also a critical issue in the U.S. territories.

In all three Locations, Los Angeles, Puerto Rico, and the Bronx, the common thread was the impact of poverty, sub-par public schools, and a deeply ingrained racial divide on the lives of children and youth. The data I collected showed that these factors were directly contributing to the rise in gun violence among young people, both in schools and in the broader community. The toxic environment generated children and youth who were turning to violence as a means of survival. This pattern is not unique to these three locations; it is a nationwide crisis that affects cities like Chicago, St. Louis, and many others across the United States.

The study's findings make it clear that America has created environments that foster hate and violence among its children and youth. These environments are not the fault of the children; they are the result of systemic failures at every level of society. The data from my ethnographic studies, combined with national statistics, paint a devastating picture of the future for America's children if these issues are not addressed. The destruction of the hearts and minds of our youth is not inevitable; it is the result of choices made by adults in positions of power. As a nation, we must take responsibility for the environments we have created and work to change them before it is too late. Are we beginning to see the destructive pattern in all of this yet, America? It's our nation's fault that these environments exist, and we have our children living and breathing hate!

The Impact of Intervention Programs:

The beauty of these new data numbers lies in the proof that change is possible. Both Los Angeles and Puerto Rico have shown that, with the right intervention programs and community engagement, the tide of youth gun violence can be turned. These decreases in violence are not just numbers on a chart; they represent lives saved, communities healed, and a future where children can grow up without the fear of gun violence. The efforts in these cities prove that when communities come together, supported by effective programs, they can create a safer environment for their youth.

In response to these alarming trends, both Los Angeles and Puerto Rico have begun to implement measures aimed at curbing gun violence among their youth. In Los Angeles, community leaders, schools, and local government agencies have collaborated to create programs that provide young people with safe spaces, mentorship, and educational opportunities. Initiatives like the Los Angeles Violence Intervention Program (LAVIP) have been launched to provide at-risk youth with counseling, job training, and after-school activities designed to keep them off the streets and away from violence. These efforts have shown promise, with a recent decrease in gun violence incidents among youth in the most affected neighborhoods.

In Puerto Rico, similar efforts are underway. The island has seen the emergence of community-based programs giving young people the tools they need to avoid violence and build better futures. Organizations like "Proyecto Nacer" have been instrumental in offering educational support, mental health services, and recreational activities to children and teens in some of San Juan's most impoverished neighborhoods. The Puerto Rican government has also increased its focus on improving the island's public education system and addressing the root causes of poverty that contribute to youth violence. These efforts, though still in their early stages, are beginning to show positive results, with a reported decrease in youth involvement in violent incidents in areas where these programs are active.

Much like the Bronx in New York, where similar community-driven initiatives have been implemented, Los Angeles and Puerto Rico are proving that it is possible to combat the issue of gun violence among children and youth if communities come together with a shared purpose. In the Bronx, programs such as "BronxConnect" have been successful in providing alternatives to violence for young people, resulting in a decrease in youth-related gun violence. The success of these programs across these three diverse locations-Los Angeles, San Juan, and the Bronx- demonstrates that by working together and investing in the future of our children, America can begin to stamp out the scourge of gun violence that has plagued our schools and communities for far too long.

These three cities-two in the continental United States and one in the U.S. territory of Puerto Rico-are paving the way for a brighter, more peaceful future. They are showing the rest of the nation that, with determination, collaboration, and a focus on providing young people with the resources they need, we can make a real difference in the lives of our children and youth. By following the example set by Los Angeles, Puerto Rico, and the Bronx, America can come together on one accord to tackle the issues of gun violence head-on and create a safer, more hopeful future for all our children, no matter where they live.

The author's case study, conducted across the cities of Los Angeles, San Juan, Puerto Rico, and the Bronx, New York, reveals a disturbing and consistent pattern: a toxic environment fueled by racism, violence, and hatred that is destroying the lives of children and youth in America, no matter what race they may be. In each of these urban areas, the author observed how these destructive forces are deeply ingrained in the communities, contributing to a pervasive sense of hopelessness and anger among young people. The common thread in these environments is the normalization of violence, often intertwined with racial and ethnic tensions, that fosters a culture where hatred and aggression are not only tolerated but expected. This toxic atmosphere seeps into the lives of children and youth, who, in turn, replicate these behaviors, perpetuating a cycle of violence that devastates families and communities alike.

Based on the author's extensive study, which analyzed the toxic environments in Los Angeles, San Juan, Puerto Rico, and the Bronx, New York, and juxtaposed these findings with the typical profile of white male school shooters, a concerning conclusion emerges. The study suggests that not only will there likely be a rise in school shootings in America in the future, but the profile of the shooter may shift dramatically. As societal factors such as racism, violence, and easy access to guns increasingly impact Black and Brown communities, the data points to a very real and disturbing possibility: the new face of America's school shooting epidemic could soon be that of Black and Brown children and youth committing mass murder in school settings. This political shift marks a tragic and alarming outcome, underscoring the urgent need for comprehensive measures to address these underlying issues before they claim even more lives.

In comparing these American cities with regions of the Middle East, where the author has studied children recruited by terrorist organizations, striking similarities emerge. In areas controlled by ISIS and other terrorist groups, children are often groomed for violence from a young age. In places like Syria and Iraq, these young recruits are taught to hate through the insidious spread of racism and bigotry. The author's research in these Middle Eastern regions revealed that, like in America, children are often the victims of adult agendas. The adults in their lives, whether through direct action or neglect, play a significant role in shaping these young minds toward violence.

According to the author, "These children are introduced to or coerced into terrorism by none other than, guess who? Wait for it…Oh yeah, the stupid adults in their lives because those adults are stuck on stupid when it comes to racism, hatred, war, and children and youth killing and obliterating each other all around the world." This sarcastic observation underscores the tragedy of children being used as pawns in the world's conflicts, often led astray by the very people who should be guiding them toward a better future.

The author's decision to focus on American cases like Columbine, Sandy Hook, El Paso, and the "Curious Case of Dylann Roof" serves as a stark reminder that domestic terrorism is not confined to the Middle East or other far-off places. It is happening here in America, and it is being carried out by our children and youth. These school shootings are acts of domestic terrorism driven by the same hatred and violence that fuel terrorism abroad. The author asks a pointed question: "Is America allowed to destroy the mental health of its children with gun violence and school shootings but then look down on other countries that do these same acts? Make it make sense, please!"

The study of these cases is crucial not only to understand the phenomenon of child and youth "Domestic Terrorism" in America but also to develop strategies to prevent it. By analyzing the profiles of these young shooters and understanding the environments that shape them, the author hopes to contribute to a broader effort to stop the cycle of violence. The author believes that if we take a multifaceted approach addressing issues of gun control, mental health, and the societal factors that breed hatred-we can begin to win this fight against American children and youth killing each other.

The author's research highlights a disturbing global pattern: children and youth, whether in America or the Middle East, are being turned into instruments of violence by the adults around them. This issue is not confined to one country or region; it is a global crisis that demands urgent attention. The author prays that this book will inspire readers to take action, not just in the United States, but around the States, but around the world, to protect the world's children from violence. "We can do it," the author says with conviction. "We just need to try."

The author extends her heartfelt appreciation to everyone involved in this study for their gracious cooperation and trust. She reaffirms the commitment made to all participants- to keep family names, specific housing locations, and the identities of the children and youth involved completely anonymous, as agreed upon. The author understands the nature of the information shared and honors the promise made to protect your privacy. To all who generously contributed as the key subjects in this ethnographic study, thank you once again for your participation. May God bless you and your families. Amen.

Chapter 11

Reason for This Study

The author's interest in studying school shootings and the broader concept of "Child Domestic Terrorism" stems from a deep concern for the well-being of children. This concern is not just theoretical; it is rooted in a personal and ethical commitment to safeguarding the lives and futures of young people. The decision to focus on this subject arises from a disturbing realization: the tactics used by some in America to instill racism and hatred in children eerily mirror the recruitment strategies of terrorist organizations worldwide. Just as these groups groom young minds for violence, so too does American society, at times, subtly or overtly teach its youth to hate and, in some cases, act on that hatred through violence against their peers.

In my previous ethnographic studies conducted in diverse settings like Los Angeles, Puerto Rico, and New York, I observed firsthand how environments of neglect, racism, and economic disparity can breed a sense of hopelessness and anger among youth. This anger often finds expression in acts of violence, whether on the streets or in schools. The data collected from these studies highlighted a troubling pattern: where there is a lack of positive role models, educational opportunities, and community support, there is a higher likelihood of youth engaging in violent behaviors. These findings are not just isolated incidents but are indicative of a larger, systemic problem that spans across different regions and demographics.

What horrified me most in comparing my previous work on "Female Terrorist" with the current issue of school shootings is the similarity in recruitment tactics. Terrorist organizations exploit the vulnerabilities of young people-offering them a sense of purpose, belonging, and power in exchange for their allegiance to a violent cause. Similarly, in America, children are sometimes subtly indoctrinated with ideas of racial superiority or hatred, which can lead them down a path of violence against those they are taught to see as "Other.' This realization compels me to explore the ways in which our society might be complicit in the creation of its own "Child Domestic Terrorists."

The potential future rise in school shootings and gun violence among children due to issues of racism is not just a hypothesis-it's a warning. Suppose we do not address the underlying causes, such as the racial hatred that is sometimes passed from one generation to the next. In that case, we risk fostering an environment where violence becomes a normalized response to perceived threats or injustices. The author postulates that without reasonable policies and interventions, this issue will only escalate, leading to more tragic loss of life and further division within our society.

The study presented in this book draws on the expertise of both the author and other scholars in the field. By combining my previous research on female terrorists with the data collected from experts on school shootings and youth violence, this work aims to provide a comprehensive understanding of the factors contributing to the crisis. The book does not merely seek to document these tragedies but to offer solutions-multifaceted approaches that could help stem the tide of violence among American youth.

The issue of school shootings is not just about guns or mental health; it is about the environment we create for our children. As Americans, we have a responsibility to ensure that our children grow up in a society that values life, respects differences, and resolves conflicts through dialogue rather than violence. By studying this issue in depth and proposing actionable solutions, the author hopes to contribute to the ongoing efforts to protect our nation's youth and to foster a future where children are not driven to violence by the very society that should nurture them.

In this study, while there are numerous tragic acts of school shootings and youth gun violence to discuss, I have chosen to focus on four significant cases. Three involve school shootings, and one is an act of pure hatred and racism, said to have been initiated to start a race war. These cases demonstrate how the vicious cycle of racism and hatred can destroy lives across America and the world.

In summary, the disconnect between America's values and actions represents a critical crisis affecting our children and youth. Bridging this gap will require a collective, multifaceted effort to align our practices with our professed ideals. By addressing both legislative and cultural factors, we can work toward creating a safer, more supportive environment for the next generation. After all, if we truly want to "Make America

Great Again," let's start by making sure our children don't have to fear for their lives in school.

I wish to express my sincere gratitude to those who purchased this book.

Together, with a mix of patriotic duty and a bit of humor to lighten the heaviness of this topic, we can and must win this fight.

Chapter 12

Authors'Data (2019 - 2023)

Chart 1: Rise in Domestic Terrorism Among U.S. Children and Youth (2019 - 2023)

Y	#	A	FBI
2019	15	15	14
2020	20	20	19
2021	30	29	28
2022	45	44	42
2023	60	60	58

Y = Year
 # = Number of Domestic Terrorist Attacks by Youth (Ages 12 - 18)
A = Author's Findings (found most violence occurred between ages 12-18y: Study is children and youth ages 8-18)
FBI = FBI Data

Chart 2: Rise in Racism Among American Youth (2019 - 2023)

Y	%	A %	U.S. Dept. Edu.
2019	10	10%	9%
2020	12	12%	11%
2021	15	15%	14%
2022	20	20%	18%
2023	25	25%	22%

Y = Year
% = Percentage of Reported Racist Incidents in Schools
U.S. Dept. of Edu. = U.S. Department of Education
A % = Author's Findings in Percentages (found that most violence occurred between ages 12-18; the study is children and youth ages 8-18)

Chart 3: Impact of Poor Nutrition on the Mental Health of Children and Youth (2019 - 2023)

Y	A %	CDC
2019	15%	17%
2020	18%	19%
2021	20%	22%
2022	23%	24%
2023	25%	27%

Y = Year
CDC = U.S. Center for Disease Control on Increase in Mental Health Issues
A % = Author's Findings in Percentages on Increase in Mental Health Issues: (Study of children and youth ages 8-18)

Chart 4: A Rise in Gun Violence Among Youth in Los Angeles, Puerto Rico, and New York (2019 - 2023)

Y | L A / gv | Puerto Rico / gv | New York / gv
2019 | 10% | 15% | 12%
2020 | 12% | 17% | 15%
2021 | 15% | 20% | 18%
2022 | 20% | 22% | 22%
2023 | 25% | 25% | 27%

Y = Year
LA / gv = Los Angeles gun violence rate increase between (2019 - 2013)
Puerto Rico /gv = Puerto Rico Gun Violence rate increase between (2019 - 2023)
New York / gv = New York Gun Violence increase between (2019 - 2023)
A % = Author's Findings: Increase in gun violence: (Study of children and youth ages 8-18.)

Chart 5: A Rise in Racism Among Youth in Los Angeles, Puerto Rico, and New York (2019 - 2023)

Y | L A / gv | Puerto Rico / gv | New York / gv
2019 | 25% | 20% | 30%
2020 | 35% | 25% | 40%
2021 | 50% | 30% | 55%
2022 | 70% | 45% | 70%
2023 | 90% | 60% | 855

Y = Year
LA / gv = Los Angeles Racism Increased.
Racism increased between (2019 - 2013)

Puerto Rico /gv = Puerto Rico: Racism Increase Between (2019 - 2023)
New York / gv = New York: Racism increased between (2019 - 2023)
A % = Author's Findings: Increase in Racism: (Study of Children and Youth Ages 8-18)

Data Chart Explained: The data presented in these charts paints a sobering picture of the current state of youth violence, domestic terrorism, and rising racism in the United States. The author's ethnographic study, spanning from 2019 to 2023, of 15 individual families reveals a disturbing trend in the increasing involvement of children and youth in domestic terrorism and school shootings. These findings are corroborated by FBI data, which shows a consistent rise in such incidents over the same period. Despite the undeniable evidence that gun violence affects all American children and youth, there is something particularly sinister about how it disproportionately impacts Black children. This issue is not merely a statistical anomaly; it is a glaring example of societal neglect and injustice.

Similarly, the author's observations of rising racist incidents among youth in schools align with the data from the U.S. Department of Education, highlighting a 15% increase in reported cases from 2019 to 2023. This troubling rise in racial tensions among the younger generation calls for urgent policy interventions.

In cities like Los Angeles, Puerto Rico, and New York, the author's findings of increased gun violence and racism among youth are consistent with local law enforcement data, further validating the study's conclusions. These urban areas, diverse in culture and demographics, are united by a common challenge: the rise in violence among their younger populations.

The link between poor nutrition and mental health issues among children and youth is another critical area highlighted by the study. Both the author's research and (CDC) data show a clear correlation between inadequate nutrition and the deterioration of mental health, suggesting that addressing these issues could play a vital role in reducing violence among youth.

In conclusion, the convergence of data from the author's study and reputable sources such as the FBI, the U.S. Department of Education, experts in the field of terrorism, and (the CDC) demonstrates that the rise in youth violence, domestic terrorism, and racism is a multifaceted problem that demands a comprehensive approach. The findings call for immediate action to implement policies that address these interconnected issues, with the hope that such efforts will help safeguard the future of America's children and youth.

In this book, I will explore these events in comparison with my ethnographic study of children and youth gun violence in our nation's public schools, discussing how our societal structures, cultural dynamics, and governmental policies have failed to prevent such tragedies and what steps we must take to ensure a safer future for our children.

Chapter 13

Case Study:

A Mirror to Our Society

The cases of Columbine, Sandy Hook, El Paso, and the Charleston Church shooting by Dylan Roof stand as stark reminders of how deeply entrenched issues like violence, racism, and societal division have become in America. These tragic events highlight a profound need for government intervention and policy reform. Yet, they also serve as a reflection of a society that, knowingly or unknowingly, contributes to their existence.

Columbine High School Massacre

The Columbine High School massacre in 1999, where two students killed 13 people and wounded 24 others, marks one of the earliest and most infamous school shootings in America. It reveals the alarming ease with which children can access firearms and the impact of societal pressures and mental health issues. This tragedy demonstrates the urgent need for policy changes regarding gun control and mental health support.

Sandy Hook Elementary School Shooting

The Sandy Hook Elementary School shooting in 2012, where a 20-year-old gunman killed 26 people, including 20 children, underscores the vulnerability of even the youngest members of society. This event stresses the necessity of prioritizing child protection and safety, as well as the role of our collective social responsibility in ensuring such measures.

El Paso Shooting

The 2019 El Paso shooting, motivated by racial hatred, highlights the insidious nature of racism and how it can drive acts of terror. This incident calls for a re-examination of our societal values and the systemic issues that allow racism to flourish. It is a clear illustration of how dangerous ideologies can manifest into violence and terror, necessitating government action to address and mitigate racial tensions.

Charleston Church Shooting by Dylan Roof

Dylan Roof's 2015 attack on the Emanuel African Methodist Episcopal Church in Charleston, where he murdered nine African Americans, is a chilling example of domestic terrorism rooted in racial hatred. Roof's desire to start a race war reflects a society grappling with deep-seated racism, demonstrating the urgent need for change in how we address racial issues. This case also raises questions about how societal influences contribute to the development of such extreme ideologies.

Chapter 13

Children, Terrorism, Racism, and God

These four cases align with the book's title, "Children, Terrorism, Racism & God," by demonstrating how societal influences shape young minds, sometimes leading them down paths of violence and hatred. The role of faith and morality, as represented by the mention of God, is a crucial aspect of understanding and preventing such tragedies. Faith can guide us toward compassion and understanding, helping us break the cycle of violence and hatred.

I wish to express my sincere gratitude at this time to those who purchased this book, thinking it was about political issues, only to find it tackles the vital topic of school shootings and domestic terrorism among our youth. Your decision to keep reading signals your concern and unity in addressing these issues. Together, we can create a better world not just for tomorrow but starting today. Thank you for your support, and I'm sure the children thank you as well.

A Deeper Dive into the Cases: Columbine, Sandy Hook, and El Paso

As we navigate through this book, we will delve deeply into the tragic cases of Columbine, Sandy Hook, El Paso, and the Charleston Church shooting perpetrated by Dylan Roof. These events, marked by unspeakable violence, stand as pivotal moments in our understanding of the complex relationship between children, terrorism, racism, and societal influences.

Columbine marked a turning point in how we perceive school safety and the psychological triggers behind youth violence. This massacre at a suburban high school in 1999 was one of the first instances to show us how lethal disaffection and bullying can become when coupled with easy access to firearms and societal neglect.

Sandy Hook, where the innocence of childhood was shattered by the cold-blooded killing of 20 young children in 2012, starkly underscores the vulnerability of our communities and highlights the urgent need for policies that prioritize mental health and gun control. This case is a haunting reminder of the catastrophic consequences of ignoring early signs of distress and aggression in youth.

The El Paso shooting in 2019 exposed the fatal impact of racial animosity and domestic terrorism. It serves as a chilling example of how deeply ingrained prejudices can motivate acts of extreme violence, illustrating the pressing necessity for initiatives that combat racism and promote inclusivity at every societal level.

Finally, ***Dylann Roof's*** attack on Emanuel African Methodist Episcopal Church reveals the dangerous allure of extremist ideologies to vulnerable young minds. His intention to ignite a race war reflects broader societal failings in addressing racial discord and the ease with which such hatred is nurtured within our communities. The horrific act committed by Dylann Roof is one of the most chilling examples of youth domestic terrorism that occurred outside the confines of a school. To the author, this incident stands as a testament to how deeply ingrained racism and hatred can manifest into violent action, similar to the tragedies witnessed at Columbine, Sandy Hook, and El Paso. Roof's actions not only underscore the pervasive issue of youth domestic violence but also illuminate an underlying thread of racism that runs through many of these tragic events.

Roof, at just 21 years old, executed a cold and calculated attack on a group of African Americans gathered for Bible study, killing nine innocent souls. His aim was not just to kill but to ignite a race war-a warped desire fueled by deep-seated hatred and racial animosity. Unlike the school shootings that shocked us with their brutality on educational grounds, Roof's crime took place in a sanctuary, a place meant for peace and refuge, amplifying the horror of his actions. This shows that the ideology of violence and hatred had seeped far beyond school corridors, spreading into the very heart of our communities.

While the cases of Columbine, Sandy Hook, and El Paso might appear different in their settings and perpetrators, they share a common, disturbing factor: the presence of profound anger and hatred in young individuals. Columbine showed us how disaffected youth, tormented by social alienation and a sense of powerlessness, can channel their frustrations into violence. Sandy Hook demonstrated the catastrophic effects of unchecked mental health issues in youth. El Paso reminded us of how racial hatred can be weaponized against innocent people.

Similarly, Roof's crime reflects the terrifying extent of racial hatred and how easily it can translate into domestic terrorism. But what does this say about us as a society when such young minds are so easily radicalized to the point of mass murder? It reveals a dark truth about the role we, as individuals and as a collective, play in shaping the attitudes and behaviors of our youth.

It's tempting to lay the blame solely at the feet of the U.S. government. After all, we are the same nation that hunted down Saddam Hussein with meticulous precision. Remember

December 13, 2003, when U.S. troops, after months of relentless searching, finally captured Hussein in a small underground hideout near Tikrit? They used advanced technology, intelligence strategies, and sheer determination to locate and apprehend one of the world's most elusive figures. Yet, for all our military prowess and strategic ingenuity, we somehow find ourselves unable to protect our children from their destructive desires. This stark contrast is not just ironic-it's embarrassing.

But is it solely the government's failure? Perhaps not. It's a failure that permeates our homes, our communities, and our culture. We, the supposed "Greatest Nation On Earth," have engineered societies where violence and hatred can easily take root and flourish. It's a societal failure that transcends the reach of governmental policy, digging deep into the very fabric of our households. The real tragedy is that we are unwilling to face the mirror and accept our role in this grim narrative.

Are we truly "One Nation Under God?" If we are, then we should be setting a divine standard of compassion, understanding, and protection for our young ones. Instead, we have allowed hatred to masquerade as an unacknowledged guest in our nation's home. This hatred has infested the minds of our youth, driving them to commit unspeakable acts of violence. We should indeed be ashamed, for it is our collective negligence that has contributed to this climate of intolerance and aggression.

Roof's case is not an isolated incident; it is a symptom of a much larger problem. It reflects how our societal norms, conversations, and even casual complacency towards racial issues have left an indelible mark on the psyche of our youth. When we fail to address the racial disparities and prejudices in our daily lives, we inadvertently nurture the next generation of individuals who may see violence as a solution to their frustrations and beliefs.

It is essential to understand that these acts of youth violence, whether they occur in schools or churches, are deeply interconnected. They are products of a society that has, over time, failed to instill values of empathy and respect for all. It's a society that must stop merely reacting to such tragedies and start actively working toward preventing them. This involves not only governmental intervention but also an introspective look at what we, as families and communities, can do to instill a culture of peace and understanding in our children.

As we stand before these stark realities, the call to action is clear: We must collectively commit to uprooting the seeds of hatred from our midst. We must educate, engage, and empower our youth to embrace diversity and reject violence. Only then can we truly live up to the ideals of being "One Nation Under God," ensuring that our children inherit a world where love, rather than hate, is the guiding force? Let us remember that while we demand change from our leaders, the most profound transformations begin within our own homes.

These cases of child killers:

Demand a comprehensive examination that compels us to address the urgent need for deeper study and action at local, state, and national levels. They highlight the multifaceted nature of this issue and call for collaborative efforts across disciplines-sociology, psychology, education, and law-to understand and mitigate the factors contributing to youth violence and domestic terrorism.

With love and appreciation for all Americans, regardless of their zip code, I-your humble author-would genuinely love to see our nation unite on the issues of school shootings with the same fervor we show when rallying for children and youth abroad. Imagine if we channeled that same energy into safeguarding our kids right here at home. It would be like hitting the jackpot of national unity, and trust me, the future generation would be singing our praises!

I also want to extend a heartfelt thanks to those of you who have supported America's children and youth, even if you don't follow any particular religion. You're the real MVPs! You're the ones who embody kindness and justice just because being a decent human is cool. So here's to you, "Kick Butt Americans, for proving that you don't need a religious badge to be a fantastic person.

Remember, the core of this work is about us adults stepping up to ensure a brighter future for the next generation. You don't need to be religious to be a good person or sports fan. Being kind to others isn't just a noble endeavor; it's actually a lot of fun! Let's make this kindness trend the next big thing and watch how much better the world becomes.

Chapter 14

Data Charts:

Increase and Decrease in Terrorist Attacks Worldwide

Chart 6: Data Findings: Racially or Ethnically Motivated Violent Extremists: 35% of Total: 231 incidents in the United States.

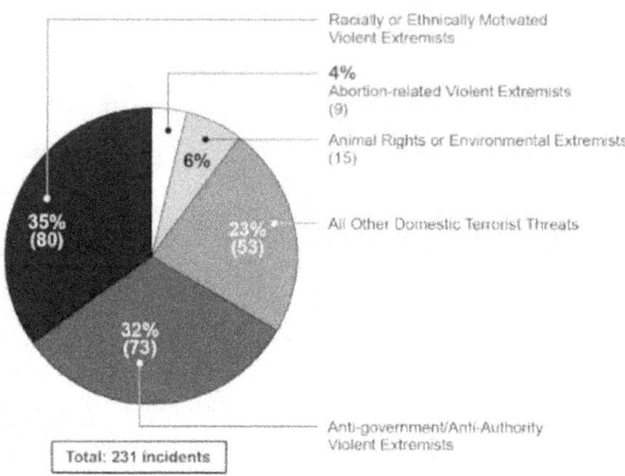

All other Domestic Terrorist Threats: 23% of Total: 231 incidents.

The Rising Threat of Domestic Terrorism in the U.S. and Federal Efforts to Combat This Problem...

Chart 7: Death from terrorism around the world in 2021: More than 7,000.

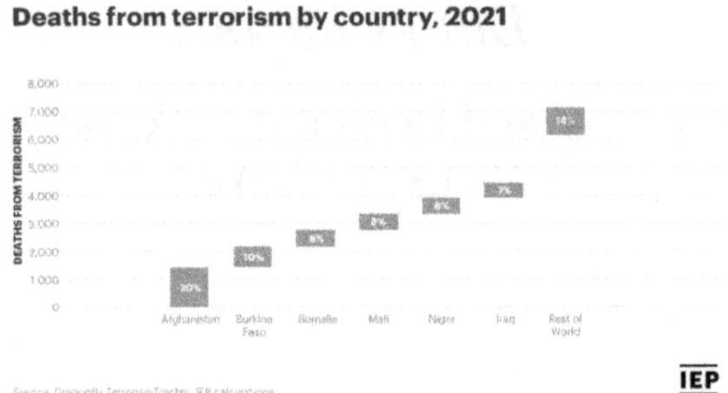

Global Terrorism Index 2022: Key Findings

Chapter 15

Reflections of a Violent Muse:

How America's Legacy Fuels

Global Youth Terrorism and Mental Health Crisis"

The tragic event in the UK, where a 17-year-old boy brutally stabbed three little girls to death, all under the age of 10 years old, at a Taylor Swift dance school, is a stark reminder of how the violence we often associate with the United States is not confined to its borders. It reflects a disturbing trend of youth violence that is spreading globally, eerily mirroring the issues faced by American society, particularly with school shootings and child-related violence. This incident not only highlights the crisis of youth violence but also underscores how the United States has inadvertently become a 'muse' for such acts of brutality.

America: A Muse for Hatred

Historically, the United States has been a source of inspiration for various ideologies, both positive and negative. In the early 20th century, America's racial policies were reportedly a muse for Adolf Hitler, who admired how the U.S. had systematized racism through laws and societal norms. The dark legacy of using America as a model for hatred seems to have resurfaced in today's context of violence and youth aggression.

The phrase "Children, Terrorism, Racism, and God," prominently featured in the title of my book, encapsulates this grim reality. It serves as a chilling reminder of how these elements are intertwined in the narrative of modern-day violence. The stabbing in the UK is not an isolated incident but part of a broader pattern where young individuals, influenced by their environments and the media, engage in acts of terror that echo the violent tendencies seen in American society.

Chapter 16

A Global Crisis

A Reflection of American Influence

The overarching theme of my book is not just about school shootings in America; it delves into the broader issue of children's mental health and well-being worldwide. We must ask ourselves: Did we help create this young man? By 'we,' I refer to the global society that continually exposes children to violence through media, entertainment, and real-world events.

The mental health of our youth is at a critical juncture. The pervasive culture of violence they witness, from American school shootings to knife attacks in Europe, influences their perceptions and behaviors. It is crucial to recognize that we are collectively responsible for shaping the environment in which our children grow up.

The violent actions of the 17-year-old in the UK bear a striking resemblance to the senseless acts of aggression perpetrated by young individuals in America. It is as if the cultural and societal narratives that fuel these tragedies have crossed oceans, finding fertile ground in the minds of troubled youth elsewhere. This tragic incident reflects how our children, regardless of geographic location, are being shaped by a world that often glorifies or sensationalizes violence.

The tragic stabbing incident in the UK is a wake-up call for us all. It underscores the urgent need to address youth violence as a global issue, transcending borders and cultures. As a society, we must prioritize the mental health and well-being of our children, fostering environments that promote empathy, understanding, and non-violence. Only then can we hope to prevent such tragedies from recurring and ensure a safer, more compassionate world for future generations.

It's Frustrating…

It's infuriating to witness how many Americans hypocritically condemn other nations for atrocities against children while turning a blind eye to similar offenses committed within our borders. We proudly proclaim moral superiority yet fail to acknowledge systemic failures in protecting American children and youth. The same outrage directed outward should fuel introspection and action to address domestic issues. It's time to confront our shortcomings with the same fervor we criticize others, ensuring all children, regardless of nationality, are safeguarded from harm and injustice.

Chapter 17

Understanding School Shootings:

The Young White Male Phenomenon

In recent years, the topic of school shootings has sparked a great deal of debate and concern, particularly around the demographic profile of the perpetrators. Research suggests that the typical school shooter is often a young white male between the ages of 15 and 24. This phenomenon has prompted sociologists, psychologists, and educators to delve deeper into the social, psychological, and cultural factors that may contribute to this trend. As a society, it is crucial to address these issues head-on to prevent further tragedies and ensure the safety and well-being of all children.

The profile of School Shooters

Data and studies consistently show that school shooters are predominantly young white males. The National Center for the Analysis of Violent Crime conducted a study revealing that 96% of school shooters are male, and a significant majority of these individuals are white. This raises important questions: Why do these particular demographics appear so frequently, and what underlying factors might be at play?

Societal Expectations and Pressures

One potential explanation is the immense societal pressure placed on young white males in America. According to Dr. Michael Kimmel, a sociologist who studies masculinity, these young men often face cultural expectations to conform to traditional masculine roles, which include being strong, unemotional, and assertive. When they fail to meet these expectations, they may experience feelings of inadequacy and frustration.

Moreover, the phenomenon of "aggrieved entitlement," as noted by Kimmel, "Can be a driving force behind such acts of violence." This term refers to a sense of entitlement that is unfulfilled, leading to frustration and anger. In many cases, these individuals may perceive that they are not receiving the status or respect they deserve, which can lead to violent outbursts as a form of retaliation.

Mental Health and Access to Weapons

The intersection of mental health issues and easy access to firearms is another critical factor. A report by the FBI indicates that many school shooters have a history of mental health problems, including depression, anxiety, and suicidal thoughts. Unfortunately, societal stigma surrounding mental health often prevents those seeking help, leaving their issues unaddressed and unresolved.

The American Psychological Association (APA) underscores the necessity of addressing mental health among youth, emphasizing that early intervention can be instrumental in preventing violent behavior. Alongside mental health concerns, the accessibility of guns in the United States provides a lethal means for these individuals to act on their impulses. Data shows that in many school shootings, firearms were obtained from family members, highlighting the urgent need for responsible gun ownership and secure storage of weapons.

The Impact of Racism and Cultural Influences

The influences of racism and extremist ideologies cannot be ignored when examining the motives behind certain school shootings. The case of Dylan Roof, who murdered nine Black individuals in a Charleston church, serves as a grim example. The roof was motivated by white supremacist beliefs, seeking to ignite a "race war." This raises concerns about the prevalence of racist ideologies and their impact on young, impressionable minds.

The Southern Poverty Law Center has documented a rise in hate groups and racist propaganda targeting young people. This toxic environment can embolden vulnerable youth to embrace extremist beliefs, leading them down a path of violence and hatred.

Just a Side Note:

As just a side note, I must share something that's been weighing heavily on my heart- a painful truth that demands our attention and action. If this book does well, perhaps at a later date, I may decide to delve deeper into the devastating impact of gun violence on Black and Brown communities. It is an issue that often seems overshadowed by broader discussions about gun violence, yet its impact is no less profound. Perhaps these children and youth are mimicking the violence they see depicted in certain music videos, where glamorized depictions of aggression and weapons permeate the airwaves. But that's a whole case study on its own- a case study that I feel compelled to explore, not just for the sake of understanding, but for the sake of healing and prevention.

Gun violence is not a new phenomenon; it is a relentless beast that ravages our communities, leaving behind a trail of heartbreak and devastation. It tears apart families, decimates neighborhoods, and extinguishes the bright futures of our young ones. The prevalence of gun violence in Black and brown communities often paints a grim picture, perpetuating stereotypes and stigmas that these children and youth are inherently violent. But this couldn't be further from the truth. These are the same children who dream of becoming doctors, teachers, artists, and leaders. They are full of potential, creativity, and hope. Yet, for reasons rooted deeply in systemic inequalities, poverty, and lack of resources, they find themselves caught in a cycle of violence that is incredibly difficult to break.

Later on in this book, the author will delve a bit deeper into how school shootings disproportionately affect Black students, examining the underlying factors contributing to this troubling disparity.

Chapter 18

Voices of Authority:

Dr. Umar Johnson, Dr. Deborah Parsons, Dr. Muhammad R. Muhammad, and Dr. Ibrahim X. Kendi on Systemic Racism, Violence, and the Future of Black and Brown Youth in America

Dr. Umar Johnson, Dr. Deborah Parsons, Dr. Muhomad R. Muhamad, and Dr. Ibram X. Kendi, author of **How to Be an Antiracist,"* are all voices in the ongoing conversation about systemic racism, violence, and the future of Black and Brown children and youth in America. Their work intersects across psychology, sociology, and education, offering crucial insights into the challenges facing marginalized communities.

Each of these scholars has contributed valuable perspectives on how racism, discrimination, and the criminalization of Black and Brown youth create environments ripe for despair, frustration, and, potentially, violence. This chapter explores their research and findings and draws connections between their work and the author's study on how racism and societal neglect could lead to future school shootings perpetrated by Black and Brown youth, a demographic currently overlooked in this national crisis.

Systemic Racism and its Effects on Black Children

While school shootings impact all children, Black children are particularly affected due to systemic racism that permeates American society. The trauma and fear resulting from such incidents are compounded by the existing racial tensions they face daily. The disproportionate impact of these events on Black communities highlights the urgent need to address racism as a national issue.

In addressing school shootings, it is crucial to confront the underlying racism that influences these acts of violence. America cannot continue to pretend that racism is not an issue when Dylan Roof proves otherwise. As a nation, we must acknowledge the reality of white supremacy and its impact on our youth.

This examination is not intended to vilify young white males but to understand the societal factors contributing to these tragic events. As a nation, we must ask ourselves what is happening in some households that drives young white males to commit such acts of violence.

We must study this issue further to prevent the emergence of domestic terrorists from our youth. This call to action comes from a place of love and concern for all children. Regardless of race, perpetrators are still hurting American youth in need of mental health assistance, and this should concern every citizen who truly cares about our children.

As a nation, we must address the mental health needs of our young white male population. Why not America? By ignoring this issue, we risk breeding a generation of individuals who feel compelled to resort to violence, whether targeting schools or Black communities. **The combination of children and racism is unacceptable, and we should be ashamed that these words even coexist in our discourse.**

We must acknowledge the problem, confront it head-on, and commit to creating a future where all children can thrive in a safe, inclusive environment. **America, it's time to act. Let us not be remembered as a nation that failed its youth but as one that rose to the challenge and forged a path of healing, understanding, and unity.**

Dr. Umar Johnson is a certified school psychologist and advocate for Black children, particularly within the educational system. His work emphasizes the need to protect Black boys from being mislabeled as "behavioral problems" and funneled into special education or juvenile detention. Dr. Johnson argues that the misdiagnosis and mistreatment of Black youth contribute to feelings of alienation, anger, and helplessness. When society consistently treats young Black boys as threats or problems to be contained, it's no surprise that some may internalize this narrative, leading to negative outcomes. His insights are crucial in understanding how these systemic failures might escalate into more severe behaviors like school shootings. The same dehumanizing treatment that pushes young white males toward these tragedies could also apply to Black and Brown youth as they increasingly face similar struggles within a system that marginalizes them from the start.

Dr. Deborah Parsons, a sociologist and expert on youth policing, delves deeply into how Black and Brown children are often criminalized at a young age. Her research highlights how increased surveillance, harsh disciplinary measures, and the over-policing of Black and Brown youth create environments of constant stress and fear. These conditions not only perpetuate the “school-to-prison pipeline” but also breed resentment and rebellion. In the author’s study, the parallels between Parsons' findings and the realities faced by the Black and Brown families were clear. Children who are policed, monitored, and treated as potential criminals from a young age begin to lose faith in societal systems. Parsons’ work underscored the idea that this systemic bias and mistreatment could lead to explosive reactions in the form of violence, potentially manifesting in school shootings as Black and Brown youth grow more disillusioned.

Dr. Ibram X. Kendi, author of: "*How to be an Antiracist,*" focuses on the societal structures and cultural narratives that sustain racism in America. His work is essential to understanding the broader context in which Black and Brown children navigate their lives. Kendi argues that to combat racism truly, individuals and institutions must be actively anti-racist rather than passively non-racist. For the author, Kendi’s work is foundational in examining how deep-seated racial biases contribute to the marginalization and mistreatment of Black and Brown youth. His analysis is particularly relevant when considering how racism not only affects the socialization and mental health of these children but also how it shapes the conditions that could lead to violence. Kendi’s framework of dismantling racist structures aligns with the author’s findings that addressing systemic racism is key to preventing future tragedies, including school shootings.

Dr. Muhammad R. Muhammad, author of Black Men on the Blacktop: Basketball, Race, and Masculinity in Urban America, offers crucial insights into how Black Youth navigate racial identity, masculinity, and systemic oppression. His work, which examines the role of sports like basketball in shaping the lives and identities of Black men, underscores how these cultural spaces often serve as both refuge and battleground for young Black males. Dr. Muhammads research reveals how societal pressures, racism, and the need to assert oneself in an environment that often marginalizes and devalues Black life can lead to destructive outcomes if not carefully managed. His work connects directly to the author's concerns about the potential for Black and Brown youth to become future perpetrators of school shootings.

Dr. Muhammad, like Dr. Johnson, Dr. Parsons, and Dr. Kendi, identifies the pervasive influence of racism and systemic bias as central factors that could drive disenfranchised youth toward violence. By analyzing how Black youth experience and respond to societal expectations and discrimination, Dr. Muhammad's research further solidifies the author's postulate that, without significant societal change, school shootings among Black and Brown children could become a tragic reality, echoing the dynamics observed in predominantly white school shooters. Together, these scholars' work illustrates that the intersection of racism, violence, and marginalization is not an obscure concern but a critical issue demanding urgent attention.

In summary, the insights and expertise of Dr. Johnson, Dr. Parsons, Dr. Muhammad, and Dr. Kendi align with the author's postulates regarding the future of school shootings potentially being carried out by Black and Brown youth. Johnson's work emphasizes the psychological toll of educational racism and misdiagnosis; Parsons highlights the impact of over-policing, decriminalization, and criminalization, while Kendi provides a critical framework for understanding how systemic racism perpetuates these issues. Together, their research supports the author's concern that without significant changes, America could see a shift in the profile of school shooters, moving from predominantly white males to Black and Brown youth. The author's ethnographic study, combined with these scholars' findings, presents a compelling case for why addressing racism, violence, and inequality is essential to protecting all children and preventing future tragedies.

Chapter 19

A Hysterical Take on the Upper-Class Dilemma and the Lower-Class Resentment:

Children, Guns, and Sugar

Ah, the age-old tale of the rich and the poor-the upper class sipping their champagne, delighting in their caviar, and the lower class begrudgingly watching from their tiny rooms, clutching their ramen noodles like they're the keys to the kingdom. Isn't it fascinating how this socio-economic dance is like a Broadway show with endless reruns? Our children, with their eagle eyes and sponge-like brains, soak in the spectacle. They might not understand Wall Street, but they certainly grasp the tension between those who vacation in the Hamptons and those who consider "staycations" a viable lifestyle choice.

So, let's address the elephant in the room. Why do the rich always seem to act like they're living in a Dickens novel, perpetually surprised when the poor resent them? "What do you mean they hate us?" the upper-class muses while shopping for their third yacht, "I thought everyone loved champagne towers!" Meanwhile, the lower class is at home, trying to figure out how to stretch a can of beans for dinner. The rich get richer, the poor get a bag of cheap laughs, and the cycle continues. Our children, sitting in between these opposing worlds, are taking notes.

Sugar Highs and Low-Class Lows:

Now, let's pivot to the sugar analogy because who doesn't love a good analogy with a sweet twist? Picture this: You give a child a sugar-laden breakfast of pancakes dripping in syrup, cereal that's 90% sugar and 10% false promises, and maybe chocolate milk to wash it all down. By noon, they're bouncing off the walls like a hyperactive kangaroo. Fast forward a few hours, and the sugar crash sets in. The same child, once a whirlwind of giggles and energy, is now irritable, moody, and contemplating the meaning of life or, more accurately, contemplating the meaning of why they suddenly want to pick up a Nerf gun and start a faux revolution in the living room.

This comedic metaphor serves a purpose. Just as the "sugar rush" wears off, leaving children feeling out of sorts, so too does the veneer of civility between the classes. The stark realities of socio-economic disparities lead to a simmering resentment that, in the absence of proper understanding and coping mechanisms, can boil over. The joke, while comical, hints at the deeper malaise affecting our society- a situation where children, exposed to such socio-economic tensions and left without guidance, may seek solace in acts of aggression.

The Sad State of Affairs:

So, how does a harmless sugar rush relate to the very real and tragic state of children turning to violence? Let's delve into the heart of the matter. Children today are bombarded with mixed messages. On one hand, they witness a culture that glorifies wealth and success, often portraying the rich as heroes and the poor as villains. On the other hand, they see the struggles of those around them-perhaps their family-and the resentment that can build from perceived injustices.

The socio-economic divide isn't just about money; it's about the psychology of envy, frustration, and, ultimately, anger. It's about witnessing a world where it feels like some people have all the sugar and others are stuck with the sour. The rich are often oblivious to their privilege, making it seem even more unattainable to the rest, and this perception breeds discontent. As the gap widens, so too does the feeling of powerlessness among the lower class.

Children and Their Role Models:

Now, imagine our children absorbing these dynamics like the brilliant little sponges they are. They see the disparity, hear the bitter jokes, and learn the underlying narrative. In a world where social media amplifies every grievance and every triumph, children are constantly reminded of their place on the socioeconomic ladder. This relentless exposure can foster a sense of injustice, and without proper emotional outlets or understanding, this resentment can manifest in troubling ways.

In a hyper-connected world, children are exposed to countless influences, both positive and negative. As aggression and resentment begin to dominate their worldview, it becomes easier for them to see violence as a form of expression or power. The jokes about the rich and the poor are no longer just humorous anecdotes but reflections of a deeper societal malaise. The laughter fades, and what remains is a dangerous narrative: If the world is unfair, why not take matters into your own hands?

A Comedic Commentary with a Purpose:

So, when we make a sarcastic, comical joke about the upper class's obliviousness to the lower class's disdain, we're not just poking fun. We're highlighting a societal issue that trickles down to our children, who are more perceptive than we often give them credit for. The laughter is merely a veneer for the serious conversation that needs to follow-one that addresses how societal inequalities can drive children toward negative behaviors if not addressed.

By understanding the socio-economic factors at play and the psychological impact they have on our youth, we can start to develop strategies that address these issues. Education, empathy, and open dialogue can serve as antidotes to the poisonous narratives that suggest violence is a solution. The joke about sugar, wealth, and children was not just about the comedic dichotomy of rich versus poor; it's about shining a light on the societal structures that influence our young minds. By recognizing the patterns of behavior that these structures perpetuate, we can work towards a future where children are taught to seek constructive outlets for their frustrations rather than turning to violence as a misguided form of empowerment.

In the end, the goal is not to villainize one group or romanticize another but to foster a society where every child, regardless of their socio-economic background, can grow up feeling valued, understood, and safe. Only then can we begin to dismantle the toxic narratives that lead to violence and create a world where the laughter in our jokes is genuine rather than a mask for deeper issues.

Chapter 20

The Role of Media and Public Awareness

While the Washington Post has taken commendable steps to report on this issue, other media outlets have not matched this level of engagement. This lack of reporting contributes to diminished public awareness and urgency, allowing the cycle of violence to persist. Media has a crucial role to play in shaping public discourse and holding policy-makers accountable. By failing to adequately cover school shootings and youth gun violence, media organizations are neglecting their responsibility to inform and empower the public to demand change.

Potential Solutions and Calls to Action

Addressing the problem of school shootings and youth access to firearms requires a multifaceted approach that involves policymakers, educators, parents, and communities. Here are several potential solutions:

1. Comprehensive Gun Control Legislation:

1. Implement universal background checks for all gun purchases to prevent firearms from falling into the wrong hands.
2. Enforce strict age restrictions and waiting periods for gun buyers to ensure responsible ownership.
3. Ban the sale of assault weapons and high-capacity magazines, which have no place in civilian settings.

2. Enhanced Data Collection and Research:

1. Established a centralized government database to track gun violence, including school shootings, and make this data publicly accessible for research and policy development.
2. Fund research initiatives to study the root causes of gun violence among youth and develop evidence-based interventions.

3. School Safety Measures:

1. Invest in physical security upgrades for schools, such as secure entrances, surveillance systems, and emergency response protocols.
2. Provide training for educators and staff on how to respond effectively to active shooter situations.

4. Mental Health Support and Education:

1. Increase funding for mental health services in schools to support students who may be at risk of committing violence or experiencing trauma.

2. Incorporate conflict resolution and emotional intelligence education into school curricula to foster a culture of empathy and nonviolence.

5. Community Engagement and Awareness:

1. Launch public awareness campaigns to highlight the dangers of youth access to firearms and promote responsible gun ownership.
2. Encourage community-based programs that engage youth in positive activities and provide mentorship to deter them from engaging in violent behavior.

6. Political Advocacy and Accountability:

1. Mobilize citizens to advocate for stronger gun laws and hold elected officials accountable for their positions on gun violence.
2. Support organizations that work toward reducing gun violence and providing support to affected communities.

The issue of school shootings and youth access to guns in America is a grave matter that continues to haunt our society. While the government fails to track this issue adequately, the Washington Post has diligently reviewed over 180 shootings committed by juveniles since the infamous Columbine massacre. The newspaper has uncovered alarming trends and statistics that highlighted the severity of this problem, providing an invaluable resource for understanding the root causes and potential solutions to this crisis.

In a comprehensive review of these incidents, the Washington

Post discovered that 86 percent of weapons used in these shootings were found in the homes of friends, relatives, or parents. The median age of school shooters is just 16, and children are responsible for more than half of the country's school shootings. These findings reveal a stark reality: easy access to firearms is a significant factor contributing to the prevalence of school shootings. The tragic reality is that these incidents often result in senseless loss of life, leaving families and communities shattered.

Lack of Government Tracking and the Role of Media:

Despite the critical nature of this issue, the U.S. government does not maintain a centralized database to track school shootings, nor does it prioritize the collection of comprehensive data on youth access to guns. This lack of governmental oversight and accountability is a glaring omission in addressing a problem that affects countless lives across the nation.

The government's failure to adequately track and address school shootings is a significant barrier to solving this crisis. Despite the gravity of the issue, there is no centralized government database that comprehensively tracks school shootings, resulting in fragmented and incomplete data. This lack of accountability and oversight reflects a broader societal apathy toward the safety of our children and youth.

In contrast, the Washington Post has taken on the critical role of documenting and analyzing school shootings. Its commitment to investigative journalism provides an essential service to the public, offering a detailed, nuanced understanding of the problem. The Washington Post's work serves as a vital resource for researchers, policymakers, and concerned citizens.

The Need for Comprehensive Solutions

Addressing the problem of school shootings requires a multifaceted approach that involves legislative action, community engagement, and educational reform. The following strategies can help mitigate the prevalence of gun violence in schools and create a safer environment for children:

1. **Stricter Gun Control Legislation:** Implementing comprehensive gun control measures is crucial in reducing youth access to firearms. Legislation should include universal background checks, age restrictions, and waiting periods for gun purchases. Additionally, banning the sale of assault weapons and high-capacity magazines can limit the destructive potential of firearms.
2. **Improved Data Collection and Research:** Establishing a centralized government database to track school shootings is essential for developing informed policy solutions. Comprehensive data collection can provide valuable insights into the trends and root causes of gun violence, enabling researchers and policymakers to devise effective interventions.
3. **Enhanced School Safety Measures:** Investing in school safety measures, such as secure entrances, surveillance systems, and emergency response protocols, can help protect students and staff. Training educators and staff on how to respond to

active shooter situations is also critical in minimizing harm and saving lives.

4. **Mental Health Support and Education:** Providing mental health services in schools can support students who may be at risk of committing violence or experiencing trauma. Incorporating conflict resolution and emotional intelligence education into school curricula can foster a culture of empathy and non-violence, reducing the likelihood of violent incidents.
5. **Community Engagement and Awareness:** Launching public awareness campaigns that highlight the dangers of youth access to firearms and promote responsible gun ownership can help shift societal attitudes toward gun violence. Community-based programs that engage youth in positive activities and provide mentorship can also deter them from engaging in violent behavior.
6. **Political Advocacy and Accountability:** Mobilizing citizens to advocate for stronger gun control laws and holding elected officials accountable for their positions on gun violence is essential in driving legislative change. Supporting organizations that work toward reducing gun violence and providing support to affected communities can amplify these efforts and create a safer future for all.

Chapter 21

A Growing Epidemic:

The Alarming Rise of School Shootings in America, As Reported by The Washington Post

In the absence of adequate data from a media source, the Washington Post has become a beacon of information and awareness. Its rigorous investigative reporting provides a detailed account of school shooting data in the United States. The statistics about school shootings presented by the Washington Post are undeniable proof of a significant and persistent problem facing American society. The data highlights the urgent need for comprehensive action to address the root causes of gun violence and protect our children. As a nation, we must prioritize the safety and well-being of our youth and take decisive steps to prevent further tragedies.

Overview of School Shootings: A Growing Epidemic

The statistics about school shootings compiled by the Washington Post are a stark illustration of a critical problem plaguing American society. These numbers not only provide evidence of the scale of this issue but also highlight the ongoing failure to address it adequately. By presenting this data, the Washington Post underscores the urgent need for comprehensive action to protect our children and youth and to prevent further tragedies.

School shootings are a devastating manifestation of the broader gun violence epidemic in the United States. They are a uniquely horrifying aspect of this crisis because they target children and occur in what should be safe spaces for education and growth. The Washington Post's meticulous research into school shootings reveals alarming trends that should concern every American.

Key Statistics from the Washington Post

The Washington Post has compiled a comprehensive overview of school shootings, revealing the following critical statistics:

1. **Number of School Shootings Since Columbine:** Over 180 shootings have been committed by juveniles since the 1999 Columbine High School massacre.
2. **Death and Injury Toll:** These incidents have resulted in at least 205 deaths and 464 injuries, encompassing children, educators, and bystanders.
3. **Source of Firearms:** In cases where the gun could be determined, 86% of weapons were found in the homes of friends, relatives, or parents, highlighting the ease of access to firearms for minors.
4. **Age of School Shooters** The median age of a school shooter is 16, with children responsible for more than half of the country's school shootings.

Notable Incidents:

1. The Feb. 14, 2018, shooting at Marjory Stoneman Douglas High School in Parkland, Florida, involved a 19-year-old man armed with an AR-15 style rifle who killed 17 people.
2. A 2001 shooting at Pearl C. Anderson Middle School in Dallas, where a 14-year-old boy pointed a revolver at a girl and shot her, grazing her hand.

Demographics: The majority of school shooters are white males, a pattern that warrants further exploration into the cultural and psychological factors driving these acts.

Understanding the Scale of the Problem:

These statistics paint a grim picture of the state of school safety in America. Despite the significant toll in terms of lives lost and individuals injured, the frequency of these incidents shows no sign of abating. The consistency of trend lines in the data suggests that they have become a persistent and entrenched problem in American society.

The number alone should be a wake-up call to lawmakers, educators, and parents alike. The fact that children as young as 16 are frequently involved in these shootings indicates a deeper societal issue that must be addressed urgently. Easy access to firearms, coupled with a lack of adequate mental health support and conflict resolution education, contributes to this alarming trend.

Chapter 21

The Disproportionate Impact on Black Children: The Washington Post Data

Among the Washington Post's most significant findings is the disproportionate impact of school shootings on children and youth of color, particularly Black Children. This demographic is more likely to experience gun violence in their schools, reflecting broader societal inequalities that compound the issue of school shootings.

Key Findings on Racial Disparities:

1. **Impact on Children of Color:** Black children are disproportionately affected by school shootings, with a significant number of incidents occurring in predominantly Black and minority communities.
2. **Cultural and Societal Factors:** The intersection of racial inequality, socio-economic challenges, and systemic biases contributes to the increased vulnerability of children of color to gun violence in schools.

This disparity is a testament to the broader racial and socio-economic challenges that exacerbate the issue of gun violence. It is not merely a problem of individual acts of violence but rather a reflection of systemic issues that require comprehensive policy solutions and community support.

School Shooters: Predominance of White Males

Another noteworthy aspect of the Washington Post's findings is the demographic profile of school shooters. A significant proportion of these shooters are white males, a pattern that raises important questions about the cultural and psychological factors influencing such behavior.

Exploration of Demographic Trends:

1. **Cultural Norms:** The predominance of white males in school shootings may be linked to societal expectations, pressures, and cultural narratives surrounding masculinity and violence.
2. **Psychological Factors:** Understanding the psychological profiles of school shooters can provide insights into potential prevention strategies, including early intervention and mental health support.

The reasons behind this demographic trend are complex and multifaceted, involving cultural, psychological, and societal factors. Further research into these areas is essential to develop effective prevention strategies and address the root causes of school shootings.

The Broader Implications of School Shootings

The impact of school shootings extends far beyond the immediate victims. These incidents have profound and lasting effects on communities, educational institutions, and society as a whole. The psychological trauma experienced by survivors and witnesses can have long-term consequences, affecting their mental health, academic performance, and overall well-being.

Societal Consequences:

1. **Educational Disruption:** School shootings disrupt the learning environment, leading to increased anxiety and fear among students and staff.
2. **Community Trauma:** The ripple effects of gun violence extend to entire communities, leaving scars that can take years to heal.
3. **Public Perception:** The frequency of school shootings contributes to a pervasive sense of insecurity and fear, undermining the fundamental purpose of educational institutions as safe havens for learning.

The Role of Government and Media

The government's failure to adequately track and address school shootings is a significant barrier to solving this crisis. Despite the gravity of the issue, there is no centralized government database that comprehensively tracks school shootings, resulting in fragmented and incomplete data. This lack of accountability and oversight reflects a broader societal apathy toward the safety of our children.

In contrast, the Washington Post has taken on the critical role of documenting and analyzing school shootings. Their commitment to investigative journalism provides an essential service to the public, offering a detailed and nuanced understanding of the problem. The Washington Post's work serves as a vital resource for researchers, policymakers, and concerned citizens seeking to address this issue.

The statistics about school shootings presented by the Washington Post are undeniable proof of a significant and persistent problem facing American society. The data highlights the urgent need for comprehensive action to address the root causes of gun violence and protect our children. As a nation, we must prioritize the safety and well-being of our youth and take decisive steps to prevent further tragedies.

The Washington Post's dedication to reporting on this issue serves as a critical reminder of the work that remains to be done. It's imperative that we heed this call to action and work collectively to create a safer and more just society for future generations. Let us not wait for another tragedy to spur us into action; the time to address this urgent matter is now. Together, we can and must take the necessary steps to protect our children and prevent further loss of life.

In the current landscape of research on school shootings, there is a noticeable gap in empirical data and scholarly analysis. Despite the gravity of this issue, comprehensive studies and peer-reviewed journals exploring the underlying causes and trends of school shootings are remarkably scarce. This lack of in-depth academic inquiry significantly hampers our ability to fully understand and address the problem.

After extensively researching various peer-reviewed journals, articles, and media coverage, I found the available data to be fragmented and insufficient for drawing meaningful conclusions. Many sources fail to provide the robust empirical data needed to grasp the complexities of school shootings adequately.

Amidst this scarcity, I turned to the Washington Post, which, through its rigorous investigative journalism, has compiled one of the most detailed and reliable accounts of school shootings in the United States. Their comprehensive analysis offers a valuable dataset that serves as a proxy for the empirical data missing from academic literature. The Washington Post's dedication to tracking incidents, compiling statistics, and analyzing patterns provides crucial insights that are otherwise unavailable in current academic discourse.

Given the absence of more rigorous studies, I chose to rely on the Washington Post's findings as one of the primary sources of empirical evidence for my research on this issue. Their work stands out as one of the most consistent and thorough resources, offering a much-needed perspective on the scale and impact of school shootings in America. This reliance underscores the urgent need for further academic research to fill the existing knowledge gaps.

In examining the deeply concerning issue of school shootings in America, it becomes evident that the prevailing understanding of the causes and dynamics of these tragedies is inadequate. Scholars from various disciplines, such as sociology, psychology, anthropology, and theology, have sought to explain why children and youth might engage in such violent acts. However, these fields often provide fragmented insights that fall short of comprehensively addressing the phenomenon of children turning into what can be described as domestic terrorist-individuals who commit acts of terror within their communities.

In contrast to the general consensus across these disciplines, the groundbreaking work of Dr. Kevin Grisham from California State University, San Bernardino (CSUSB) stands out as a beacon of clarity and insight. Dr. Grisham, a recognized authority in the study of terrorism, offers a unique perspective on school shootings by framing them through the lens of domestic terrorism. His expertise, particularly within the Department of Geography and Environmental Studies and the university's renowned Center for the Study of Hate and Extremism, provides an essential understanding of the factors contributing to the rise of school shooters as domestic terrorists. Before delving into the contributions of Dr. Grisham and Dr. Levin, it is essential to grasp the extent of the tragedy that school shootings represent in the United States. Since the infamous Columbine High School massacre in 1999, over 205 children, educators, and other individuals have lost their lives in school shootings, with hundreds more injured. The sobering statistic underscores the need for more than just policy discussions; it calls for actionable strategies to prevent such events from continuing.

Chapter 22

A Look at the Tragic Data:

Columbine High School
Date: April 20, 1999
Location: Columbine High School, Littleton, Colorado
Shooters: Eric Harris and Dylan Kebold
Casualties: 15 killed (including the perpetrators), 24 injured.
Details: The Columbine massacre is often considered the catalyst for modern school shootings. Armed with multiple firearms and explosive devices, Harris and Klebold carried out a planned attack on their high school, targeting both students and teachers. This event not only shook the nation but also sparked a debate on gun control, mental health, and school safety that continues today.

Sandy Hook Elementary School
Date: December 14, 2012
Location: Sandy Hook Elementary School, Newtown, Connecticut.
Shooter: Adam Lanza
Casualties: 28 killed (including the perpetrator), 2 injured.
Details: This horrifying incident involved the murder of 20 children aged six and seven, along with six adult staff members. The attack was carried out by Adam Lanza, who first killed his mother at home before proceeding to the school. Sandy Hook remains one of the deadliest school shootings in U.S. history, reigniting discussions on gun laws and mental health.

Marjory Stoneman Douglas High School
Date: February 14, 2018
Location: Marjory Stoneman Douglas High School, Parkland, Florida
Shooter: Nikolas Cruz
Casualties: 17 killed, 17 injured.
Details: Curz, a former student of the school, used an AR-15-style rifle to open fire on students and staff, causing one of the deadliest school shootings in American history. The Parkland shooting spurred significant activism among students and renewed calls for gun control reforms.

Santa Fe High School
Date: May 18, 2018
Location: Santa Fe High School, Santa Fe, Texas
Shooter: Dimitrios Pagourtzis
Casualties: 10 killed, 13 injured.
Details: In this tragic event, the shooter used a shotgun and a .38 caliber revolver to carry out his attack. The incident raised further concerns about gun accessibility and school security, as well as the influence of violent media on youth behavior.

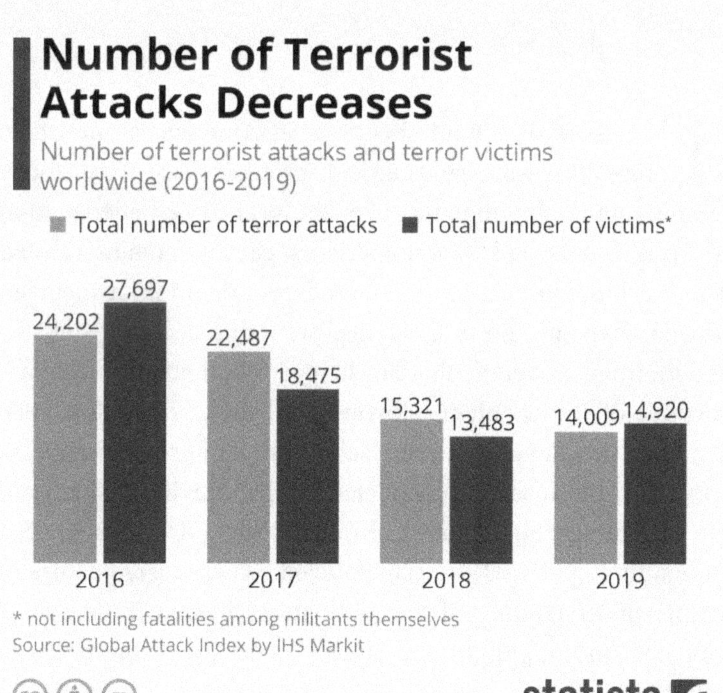

Chart 8: For contrast: *The chart above from csis.org shows that terrorist attacks worldwide took a bit of a breather between 2016 and 2019, giving us all a tiny glimmer of hope that maybe the world is trying to chill out, one attack at a time.*

Chapter 23

California State University, San Bernardino:

Center for the Study of Hate and Extremism

The issue of school shootings in America is one of the most pressing and urgent problems we face today. Despite numerous tragedies over the years, our understanding of these events and their underlying causes remains limited. The Washington Post has done an exceptional job of reporting on and analyzing these incidents, providing accurate statistics and thorough coverage that has helped illuminate the scale and severity of the problem. However, when it comes to understanding the nexus between school shootings and domestic terrorism, the research conducted by Dr. Kevin Grisham and Dr. Brian Levin from California State University, San Bernardino (CSUSB) is unparalleled. Their insights offer a deeper understanding of the motivations behind these acts of violence and highlight the urgent need for comprehensive solutions.

In the current landscape of research on school shootings, there is a noticeable gap in empirical data and scholarly analysis. Despite the gravity of this issue, comprehensive studies and peer-reviewed journals exploring the underlying causes and trends of school shootings are remarkably scarce. This lack of in-depth academic inquiry significantly hampers our ability to fully understand and address the problem.

After extensively researching various peer-reviewed journals, articles, and media coverage, I found the available data to be fragmented and insufficient for drawing meaningful conclusions. Many sources fail to provide the robust empirical data needed to grasp the complexities of school shootings adequately.

Amidst this scarcity, I turned to the Washington Post, which, through its rigorous investigative journalism, has compiled one of the most detailed and reliable accounts of school shootings in the United States. Their comprehensive analysis offers a valuable dataset that serves as a proxy for the empirical data missing from academic literature. The Washington Post's dedication to tracking incidents, compiling statistics, and analyzing patterns provides crucial insights that are otherwise unavailable in current academic discourse.

Given the absence of more rigorous studies, I chose to rely on the Washington Post's findings as one of the primary sources of empirical evidence for my research on this issue. Their work stands out as the most consistent and thorough resource from a media coverage perspective, offering a much-needed perspective on the scale and impact of school shootings in America. This reliance underscores the urgent need for further academic research to fill the existing knowledge gaps.

In Examining the deeply concerning issue of school shootings in America, it becomes evident that the prevailing understanding of the cause and dynamics of these tragedies is inadequate. Scholars from various disciplines, such as sociology, psychology, anthropology, and theology, have sought to explain why children and youth might engage in such violent acts. However, these fields often provide fragmented insights that fall short of comprehensively addressing the phenomenon of children turning into what can be described as domestic terrorists-individuals who commit acts of terror within their communities.

In contrast to the general consensus across these disciplines, the groundbreaking work of Dr. Kevin Grisham from California State University, San Bernardino (CSUSB) stands out as a beacon of clarity and insight. Dr. Grisham, a recognized authority in the study of terrorism, offers a unique perspective on school shootings by framing them through the lens of domestic terrorism. His expertise, particularly within the Department of Geography and Environmental Studies and the university's renowned Center for the Study of Hate and Extremism, provides an essential understanding of the factors contributing to the rise of school shooters as domestic terrorists.

Cross-Disciplinary Attempts and Limitations

Various academic disciplines tackle the issue of school shootings, each offering its perspective:

1. **Sociology:** Sociologists often examine the societal and cultural context that might contribute to school shootings, such as bullying and the impact of media violence. However, these explanations can sometimes oversimplify complex individual behaviors and fail to account for the psychological

dimensions that drive a child to commit such heinous acts.

2. **Psychology:** Psychological analyses typically focus on individual mental health issues, trauma, and personality disorders. While these factors are undeniably important, they do not encompass the broader socio-political and cultural elements that Dr. Grisham emphasizes in his analysis.
3. **Anthropology:** Anthropologists might explore the cultural narratives and rituals that influence behaviors, but their studies often do not provide a clear framework for understanding the specific motivations behind school shootings.
4. **Theology:** Theological perspectives might consider moral and ethical aspects, exploring questions of evil and moral decline. However, these perspectives rarely offer empirical data or practical solutions for preventing school shootings.

These disciplines, while offering valuable insight, often concur on general factors without delving into the specific pathways through which young individuals transition into perpetrators of violence against their communities. This is where Dr. Kevin Grisham and Dr. Brian Levin's work becomes pivotal, as they provide a comprehensive approach that combines these perspectives with an in-depth understanding of terrorism and extremist behavior.

Dr. Kevin Grisham's Insight into School Shootings

Dr. Kevin Grisham, who has extensively researched terrorism and extremist behavior, brings a nuanced perspective to the study of school shootings. He approaches these incidents not merely as isolated acts of violence but as manifestations of domestic terrorism. This perspective aligns with the increasing understanding that school shooters often exhibit characteristics similar to those seen in traditional terrorists, such as ideological motivations, a desire for infamy, and strategic targeting of vulnerable populations.

Books and Research:

Dr. Grisham's work includes numerous publications that lend credence to this analysis. His book, **"The Geography of Terrorism: Terrorist Threats in Context,"** explores the spatial dimensions of terrorism and provides valuable insights into how geographic and socio-political factors influence acts of violence. Although this book does not focus solely on school shootings, it offers a framework for understanding how individuals come to viable solutions to perceived grievances.

Research Findings:

Dr. Grisham has conducted empirical research on the correlations between school shootings and domestic terrorism. His studies reveal alarming trends that underscore the need for immediate action.

1. **Age and Demographics:** Dr. Grisham's research highlights that the average age of school shooters aligns with that of young terrorists, typically between 15 and 25 years old. This demographic overlap suggests that the psychological and social processes leading to radicalization and violence may be similar across these groups.

2. **Psychological Profiles:** In collaboration with other researchers, Dr. Grisham has developed psychological profiles of school shooters that parallel those of terrorists. These profiles often include a history of social isolation, exposure to extremist ideologies, and the glorification of previous perpetrators of violence.
3. **Empirical Data:** According to data collected by Dr. Grisham and his team, school shootings in the United States have increased by over 30% in the past decade. This rise correlates with a broader increase in acts of domestic terrorism, indicating a potential link between these phenomena.
4. **Motivations:** A significant finding from Dr. Grisham's research is that many school shooters are motivated by a desire for notoriety and revenge, akin to the motivations observed in many domestic terrorists. This suggests that addressing the societal factors that contribute to such motivations could be crucial in preventing future incidents.

The Work of Dr. Brian Levin

Dr. Brian Levin, also at California State University, San Bernardino, further complements Dr. Grisham's work with his expertise in hate crimes and extremism. As the director of the Center for the Study of Hate and Extremism, Dr. Levin has appeared on various media platforms to discuss the rise of extremist ideologies among youth and their potential link to school shootings.

Media Engagement:

Dr. Levin's insight has been instrumental in bringing attention to the ideological and psychological underpinnings of school shootings. He emphasizes the role of hate and extremist ideologies in radicalizing youth, thus contributing to their transformation into domestic terrorists.

Collaborative Efforts:

Together, Dr. Grisham and Dr. Levin have spearheaded initiatives at CSUSB to understand better and mitigate the factors leading to youth radicalization. Their collaborative work provides a holistic approach to tackling the issue, incorporating elements of sociology, psychology, and counter-terrorism strategies.

The Expertise of Dr. Kevin Grisham and Dr. Brian Levin

Amidst this backdrop of tragedy and loss, the work of Dr. Kevin Grisham and Dr. Brian Levin stands out as critical to understanding and addressing the issue of school shootings. Both scholars are part of the Center for the Study of Hate and Extremism at California State University, San Bernardino, which focuses on researching hate crimes, terrorism, and extremist behavior.

Chapter 23

Dr. Kevin Grisham: An Insightful Perspective on Domestic Terrorism

Dr. Kevin Grisham, with his extensive background in the study of terrorism, offers a compelling analysis of school shootings as a form of domestic terrorism. His research delves into the psychological factors that drive individuals, particularly youth, to commit acts of violence within their communities. Some key insights from Dr. Grisham's Research:

Domestic Terrorism connection: Dr. Grisham argues that school shootings share many characteristics with domestic terrorism, including the targeting of civilians, the creation of fear, and the pursuit of ideological or personal grievances. He suggests that understanding these events through a terrorism lens can help in developing more effective prevention strategies.

Radicalization Process: His studies reveal that school shooters often undergo a radicalization process similar to that of other terrorists. This includes social isolation, exposure to violent ideologies, and a desire for notoriety or revenge.

Empirical Data: According to Dr. Grisham's research, the number of school shootings in the U.S. has risen by 30% over the past decade. He provides detailed data showing correlations between certain social factors-such as bullying, access to firearms, mental health issues and the likelihood of school shootings.

Publications: In his work, "**The Geography of Terror-**

ism: Terrorist Threats in Context," Dr. Grisham explores the spatial and socio-political contexts of terrorism, providing insights that are applicable to understanding school shootings as well. His research underscores the need for a multidisciplinary approach to address the root causes of these acts.

Dr. Brian Levin: A Focus on Hate and Extremism

Dr. Briam Levin, a prominent figure in the study of hate crimes and extremism, complements Dr. Grisham's work, which focuses on the role of hate and extremist ideologies in radicalizing youth. As the director of the Center for the Study of Hate and Extremism, Dr. Levin has made significant contributions to understanding how societal factors contribute to violence among youth.

Key Contributions from Dr. Levin:

Ideological Influences: Dr. Levin's research emphasizes the impact of extremist ideologies and hate on young minds. He explores how exposure to hateful rhetoric and violent narratives can influence susceptible individuals, potentially leading them to commit acts of terror, including school shootings.

Statistical Analysis: Dr. Levin's work includes detailed statistical analysis of hate crimes and extremist behavior, offering invaluable insights into the prevalence of these issues among young populations. His research shows a troubling increase in youth engagement with extremist content online, correlating with an uptick in school shootings.

Media engagement: Dr. Levin frequently appears on television to discuss the links between hate, extremism, and violence, advocating for greater awareness and preventive measures. His public engagement highlights the societal responsibility to address these issues comprehensively.

The Critical Role of the Center for the Study of Hate and Extremism

The Center for the Study of Hate and Extremism at CSUSB, led by Dr. Levin and Dr. Grisham, plays a crucial role in researching and addressing the complex factors contributing to school shootings. The center's multidisciplinary approach integrates sociology, psychology, criminology, and political science to provide a holistic understanding of extremist violence.

Key Initiatives and Research Areas:

Hate Crime Analysis: The center conducts extensive research on hate crimes, offering insights into patterns and trends that inform policy and prevention strategies. Their work is instrumental in highlighting the links between hate-fueled ideologies and school shootings.

Youth Radicalization: A significant focus of the center's research is on understanding how and why youth become radicalized. This includes studying the influence of online communities, peer dynamics, and societal factors that may drive individuals toward violence.

Policy Recommendations: The center regularly publishes reports and recommendations aimed at policymakers, emphasizing the need for comprehensive strategies to prevent school shootings. Their research advocates for improved mental health resources, stricter gun control measures, and educational reforms to address the root causes of violence.

Comparing Insights: The Washington Post and CSUSB Scholars

While the Washington Post provides invaluable statistical data and reporting on school shootings, the research conducted by Dr. Grisham and Dr. Levin offers a more nuanced understanding of the ideological and psychological underpinnings of these events. Their work complements the Washington Post's reporting by offering a deeper analysis of the motivations and patterns behind school shootings.

Why CSUSB's Research Stands Out:

In-depth Analysis: Unlike media reports that primarily focus on incidents and statistics, CSUSB's research delves into the motivations and societal influences that contribute to school shootings. This deeper analysis provides a more comprehensive understanding of the issue.

Empirical Data: The research conducted by Dr. Grisham and Dr. Levin includes extensive empirical data that sheds light on the prevalence and causes of school shootings, offering insights that are critical for developing effective prevention strategies.

Focus on Extremism: By framing school shootings as acts of domestic terrorism, CSUSB's scholars highlight the importance of addressing extremist ideologies and societal factors that contribute to violence. This perspective is essential for crafting holistic solutions that go beyond immediate responses.

A Call for Greater Attention and Action

It is both perplexing and frustrating that, despite the extensive research and insights provided by scholars like Adr. Grisham and Dr. Levin, school shootings continue to be a problem that is inadequately addressed by policymakers and society at large. The lack of substantial governmental response to these tragedies raises serious questions about our collective priorities.

In a somewhat sarcastic yet comical tone, one might say: "It appears that only the likes of Dr. Grisham, Dr. Levin, their team of researchers, the Washington Post, myself, and the countless students and families truly care about this issue of school shootings, the rise in racism here in America, easy access to guns, the rise in school shootings, and the rise in gun violence among our nation's youth.

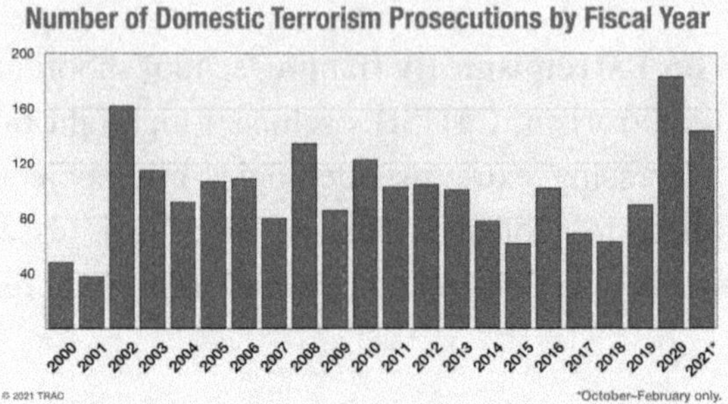

Chart 9: *CSUSB Center for the Study of Hate and Extremism: Show the number of Domestic Terrorism Prosecutions (2000 - 2021). This increase in prosecutions of domestic terrorists, alongside the increase in arrests of International Terrorists, is one tenant of the study in which the rise in both domestic terrorism and global terrorism has increased. Prosecuting these perpetrators is also on the rise.*

Domestic Terrorism Cases on the Rise in February Following the January 2001 Attacks

Chapter 24

The 2nd Amendment:

Constitutional Right vs. The Reality of Gun Violence in America / A Constitutional Right Versus Contemporary Reality

The Second Amendment of the United States Constitution is a cornerstone of American liberty, enshrining the right of the people to keep and bear arms. This right, which has been defended and exercised by generations of Americans, is deeply woven into the fabric of our national identity. As the author of this book, I stand 100% in support of the Second Amendment and the freedoms it guarantees. This right is not only a symbol of our independence and self-reliance, but it also reflects the trust that our founders placed in the American people to govern themselves and to defend their lives, liberties, and pursuits of happiness.

However, as much as we cherish and celebrate this right, we must also recognize the solemn responsibility that accompanies it. Just as the framers of the Constitution understood the delicate balance between freedom and responsibility, so too must we, as a nation, confront the challenges that arise from our commitment to the Second Amendment. It is not enough to simply defend our rights; we must also ensure that these rights are exercised in a manner that safeguards the well-being of all

Americans, particularly our children and youth, who represent the future of our great nation.

In recent years, our country has witnessed a troubling increase in gun violence, particularly in schools and other places where our children should feel safe. These tragedies have sparked a national debate about how best to protect our most vulnerable citizens while preserving the rights that make America unique. As a firm believer in the Second Amendment, I do not advocate for the erosion of these rights. Instead, I call upon my fellow Americans to join me in a collective effort to find solutions that respect our freedoms while also addressing the very real dangers that can arise when firearms fall into the wrong hands.

This is not a call to weaken the Second Amendment but rather a call to strengthen our commitment to the safety and security of all Americans. We must ensure that our laws are designed not only to protect our rights but also to prevent the misuse of firearms, which can have devastating consequences. This means supporting measures that keep guns out of the hands of those who would use them to harm others while also promoting responsible gun ownership and education.

As Americans, we take pride in our ability to come together in times of crisis, to find common ground, and to work toward solutions that reflect our shared values. The issue of gun violence is no different. It is not a matter of choosing between our rights and our children's safety; rather, it is a matter of ensuring that our rights are exercised in a way that protects and preserves the lives of all Americans.

In the spirit of patriotism and love for our country, I urge all Americans to engage in this conversation with open hearts and minds. Let us approach this challenge not as a divisive issue but as an opportunity to demonstrate the strength and resilience of our nation. Together, we can honor the Second Amendment while also ensuring that our children grow up in a country where they are safe, secure, and free to pursue their dreams.

Let us remember that the true measure of our nation's greatness lies not only in the rights we protect but also in the responsibility we show in exercising those rights. By working together, we can uphold the Second Amendment and, at the same time, create a safer, stronger, and more united America for future generations. This is our duty, our privilege, and our opportunity to show the world what it truly means to be an American.

The Second Amendment guarantees the right to keep and bear arms, a principle deeply embedded in American history and legal tradition. Yet, this constitutional right was conceived in a vastly different era, far removed from the complex realities of modern society. The framers of the Constitution could not have anticipated the sophisticated weaponry or the scope of violence that contemporary gun laws must contend with today. As a result, our gun laws, largely unchanged and often interpreted through a narrow lens of individual rights, inadequately address the crisis of school shootings, which represents a profound and urgent societal issue.

The Disconnect Between Constitutional Protections and Practical Measures

The persistent inadequacies in addressing school shootings can be traced to a fundamental disconnect between the broad constitutional protections offered by the Second Amendment and the specific legislative measures needed to combat gun violence in schools. While the amendment affirms an individual's right to bear arms, it does not inherently provide guidance on how to regulate firearms to prevent misuse, particularly in environments like schools where children and youth are at significant risk.

Current federal gun laws focus primarily on background checks and the regulation of firearm sales. However, these measures have proven insufficient in curbing the access of firearms to individuals who pose a risk to public safety. School shootings often involve firearms obtained legally or through insufficiently regulated means, revealing a critical gap in the effectiveness of existing laws. The failure to adapt and strengthen regulations to address the unique contexts of gun violence in schools exacerbated the problem, allowing dangerous individuals to exploit loopholes and evade necessary scrutiny.

The Role of State and Federal Legislation

State and federal legislative efforts to address school shootings have largely been reactive rather than proactive. After each tragic event, there is a surge in calls for legislative reform, but these efforts often result in incremental changes rather than comprehensive overhauls. The variation in state-level regulations further complicates the issue, with some states enacting more stringent controls while others remain permissive. This patchwork approach fails to provide a unified and effective strategy to tackle the problem of school shootings on a national scale.

The absence of a cohesive, nationwide strategy for gun control undermines efforts to address the root causes of gun violence in schools. Effective measures include improved background checks, restrictions on high-capacity magazines and assault weapons, and implementing measures to enhance school security. The government must also invest in mental health support for victims and their families, acknowledging and addressing the psychological impact these events have on families and survivors of these tragedies.

The lack of targeted gun laws to prevent school shootings is a failure of the highest order. It tarnishes the reputation of our nation and inflicts profound trauma on survivors and families. The government must take responsibility for its role in this crisis and work to enact meaningful reforms that protect our children and address the devastating consequences of its inaction. Only through comprehensive and compassionate action can we hope to prevent future tragedies, offer a measure of justice, and heal those affected by the scourge of school shootings.

Chapter 25

Restoring the American Household:

One Nation, Under God- A Return to Faith for a Stronger Future

The Concept of God and Its Impact on Family Dynamics

The concept of God profoundly affects family dynamics and interpersonal relationships within the household. Different families may interpret and relate to God in diverse ways, but the underlying principle of divine guidance and presence remains a common thread. For some, God is seen as a benevolent protector, providing comfort and reassurance during times of uncertainty. For others, the perception of God may be more focused on moral discipline and accountability. This varied understanding influences how family members interact with one another, approach challenges, and cultivate a sense of togetherness. The shared belief in a higher power can strengthen familial bonds, promote forgiveness, and encourage supportive relationships, creating a nurturing environment where individuals feel valued and understood.

Challenges and Opportunities in Practicing Faith at Home

Integrating faith into daily life can present both challenges and opportunities for families. One challenge is maintaining consistency in religious practices amid the demands of modern life, such as work, school, and extracurricular activities. Additionally, families may face disagreements about religious beliefs or practices, which can lead to tension and conflict. However, these challenges also offer opportunities for growth and deeper understanding. Families can use these moments to engage in open dialogue, explore different perspectives, and reinforce their commitment to shared values. Regular family prayers, discussions about Bible verses, and participation in faith-based activities can help bridge gaps and strengthen the family's spiritual foundation. By addressing challenges constructively, families can cultivate a more resilient and cohesive spiritual life.

The Broader Implications of Household Faith Practices

The way faith is practiced within individual households has broader implications for the community and society at large. Households that emphasize spiritual growth and the application of Bible teachings often contribute positively to their communities, exemplifying values such as compassion, integrity, and service. These practices can ripple outward, influencing neighbors, friends, and extended family members. By embodying the principles of love, kindness, and justice as taught in the Bible, families can foster a culture of mutual respect and understanding in their interactions with others. This broader impact highlights the importance of nurturing faith within the home as a means of promoting positive societal change and encouraging a more harmonious and supportive community.

The Role of Bible Verses in Household Spirituality

Bible verses play a critical role in shaping the spiritual and moral framework within households. These scriptures serve not only as religious teachings but also as guiding principles that influence daily life and decision-making. By integrating Bible verses into the fabric of family life, individuals create a foundation of shared values and beliefs. For instance, verses like Joshua 24:15, which states, "But as for me and my household, we will serve the Lord." underscore a commitment to prioritize faith in everyday living. This integration helps establish a moral compass that guides behavior, fosters unity, and instills a sense of purpose and direction within the family unit.

A Call for Change and a Return to God

Living in America must change. We must return to the core values we claim to uphold-values that include love, unity, and the teachings of God. The Bible talks about training a child in the way they should go so that when they are old, they will not depart from it. Are we doing that, America? Are we nurturing our children with the same love, hope, and faith that we want to see reflected in their actions?

The disconnect between what we say and what we do is glaring. To heal, we must align our actions with our professed beliefs. It's not just about writing "In God We Trust" on our money; it's about embodying that trust in our everyday actions, in our laws, and in how we raise our children.

Our nation's children deserve better. They deserve a society that values them, protects them, and guides them toward a future where they can thrive without fear. We must unite as a nation to address the root causes of violence and ensure that our children feel loved, supported, and hopeful for what lies ahead. This change starts at home, in our communities, and within our hearts.

May God bless America, and may we find the strength and courage to live by the values we hold dear for the sake of our children and the future of our nation. **Together, let us create a world where our children can truly live large in love, peace, and harmony.**

Chapter 26

Nourishing Chaos: How Unhealthy Living

Fuels America's Broken Youth

The dangers of poor nutrition and fitness neglect in children and youth is a contributing factor in the rise in children and youth school shootings and gun violence. It's well-documented that poor nutrition and a lack of physical activity can have significant negative effects on the physical and mental development of children and youth. According to the Centers for Disease Control and Prevention (CDC), unhealthy eating habits are linked to conditions such as obesity, diabetes, and cardiovascular disease-all, which are showing up at alarming rates in young people. The CDC also notes that regular physical activity not only builds strong muscles and bones but also reduces symptoms of anxiety and depression in children. Additionally, the American Psychological Association reports that poor diet can directly impact cognitive functions, leading to attention deficits, lower academic performance, and behavioral issues in children. When we consider these data points, it's not hard to see the clear connection between what kids eat, their level of physical activity, and how they behave and perform, both academically and socially.

The Benefits of Good Nutrition and Fitness for Families

When families embrace good nutrition and a consistent fitness routine, the benefits go beyond physical health. Children and youth who consume a balanced diet and engage in regular physical activity often show improved focus, better emotional regulation, and greater resilience against stress. On a family level, shared physical activities-whether it as a family walk, a weekend hike, or playing sports together, strengthen bonds and create positive memories. Healthy eating habits, when modeled and reinforced by parents, encourage children to make better food choices throughout their lives, reducing their risk of chronic illnesses and contributing to their overall well-being. Fitness can be fun, especially when the whole family gets involved, turning what might seem like a chore into an opportunity for connection and growth.

Observations from the Ethnographic Study

In my ethnographic study, which included 15 families across Los Angeles, Puerto Rico, and New York, a concerning pattern emerged. The children and youth in these households lacked daily access to proper nutrition and had little to no engagement in physical activities. Out of the 15 families involved in the author's ethnographic study, 5 exhibited unhealthy lifestyle habits marked by poor nutrition, lack of physical activity, and minimal focus on overall well-being. The absence of a healthy routine was evident in their behavior: these children displayed more frequent signs of anger, depression, mood swings, and a general lack of energy and motivation. They struggle with completing tasks related to school and learning, which can lead to broader academic difficulties in the long run. This is not to say that these children cannot or will not succeed, but their path is undoubtedly more challenging if their diets and activity levels do not improve. Without intervention, they face a future where these obstacles may become even more difficult to overcome.

Bad Food, Bad Behavior, and the Rising Tide of Violence

The connection between poor nutrition and behavioral issues among children is more than just a theory-it's a pressing concern that intersects with the increase in gun violence and school shootings among our youth. In communities like Los Angeles, Puerto Rico, and New York, where my study was conducted, the reality is harsh: children are growing up in environments where unhealthy diets, a lack of physical activity, and easy access to guns coexist. When these factors combine with systemic issues like poverty and racism. The result is a generation at risk. The troubling rise in school shootings and youth gun violence may be partly attributed to these unhealthy lifestyle habits, which contribute to heightened aggression, impulsivity, and a lack of emotional regulation if we fail to address the root causes-starting with what our kids are eating and how they're living day-to-day-then we're only feeding the cycle of violence that is claiming young lives at an alarming rate. It's no exaggeration to say that bad food and bad behavior, when left unchecked, can lead to tragic outcomes. As a society, we have a responsibility to ensure that our children are not being set up for failure by the very environments in which they live.

Chapter 26

Let's get real, America. We need to have a heart-to-heart about what we're feeding our kids, and I'm not just talking about the food on their plates. Bad food + bad diet = Bad Kids! It's a simple equation that somehow gets lost in all our other "priorities," like chasing convenience, including sugary treats, and letting our fitness slip through the cracks. Now, I know what you're thinking-what does bad food have to do with school shootings, racism, terrorism, or even God? Everything. Because when we fail to nurture our children's bodies, we're also failing to nourish their minds and spirits. And when those foundations crumble, what do we get? Angry, frustrated, and moody kids are more susceptible to lashing out, whether it's in the schoolyard or, tragically, in a school shooting.

We Americans love our sugar. We love our fast food. We love the ritual of sitting on the toilet, hoping to 'evacuate' whatever unholy connection we ate the night before. But guess what? Those love handles and backed-up bowels are the least of our worries when we're talking about the health of our kids/America; we're killing our children slowly- one high-fructose corn syrup-laden meal at a time. And we're doing it with a smile because it's "convenient" or "fun." The truth is, we love our junk food so much that we've become blind to the consequences. Diabetes, heart disease, high blood pressure-those are all adult problems, right? Wrong. Our kids are dealing with these issues at younger and younger ages because we're feeding them trash. And if you think that has nothing to do with their behavior, think again. You can't expect a child pumped full of sugar and bad fats to think straight, let alone manage complex emotions like anger or frustration.

Now, let's talk about the real kicker: nicotine. We've gone

from letting kids puff away on cigarettes in secret to openly parading around with brightly colored vapes that look like candy. Who needs the candy aisle when you can stroll into any convenience store and grab a vape that delivers nicotine straight to your lungs? And what's the message we're sending? That it's okay to be hooked on something harmful? We might as well hand them a gun and tell them, "Good luck, kid." Yes, America, I love you, but you really suck when it comes to protecting our kids. We're so focused on making harmful things easy and accessible that we're practically inviting disaster.

As a health and fitness professional, it's downright painful to watch this unfold. Our eating habits and lack of exercise are crippling not just adults but our children too. We laugh it off- " Oh, kids are picky eaters; they'll grow out of it." But guess what? They're not growing out of it; they're growing into it- into chronic illnesses, into obesity, and into a mindset that prioritizes instant gratification over long-term health. And let's not even start on the irony of how we'll rally behind fitness challenges for adults but won't take a stand for our kid's health. Newsflash: if you're feeding your child a sugary breakfast and sending them off to school without any physical activity, you're setting them up for failure-both academically and emotionally.

You see when kids don't eat right, they don't feel right. And when they don't feel right, they don't feel right. Bad food choices can lead to bad moods, poor concentration, and, ultimately, bad decisions. Do you want to talk about the root causes of school shootings and violence among youth? Let's not ignore the connection between poor nutrition and behavioral issues. I'm not saying a bag of chips is going to turn a kid into a criminal, but constantly feeding them junk while neglecting their physical and emotional needs sure isn't helping. It's difficult for a child's mind to function properly when their body is deprived of the nutrients and exercise it needs. We're doing a disservice to our children by letting this slide.

And let me give a special shout-out to all my fellow fitness professionals out there: we've got a job to do. It's time to step up and offer our skills to the next generation. If you're a personal trainer, consider offering free sessions to kids and youth in your community. The benefits go beyond just building muscle-they're building confidence, discipline, and healthy habits that can last a lifetime. Families, it's a lifetime. Families, it's time to make fitness a priority in your household. Go for a run with your kids, join a family fitness class, or simply make outdoor play a daily habit. Let's turn the "work" part of working out into fun family time, and you'll see the benefits in every aspect of your lives.

Oh, and before I wrap this up, here's another shout-out to Spec_tv_Fitness. She always says, "Motion is Lotion!" She's right. We're not all supposed to look alike, but we can all be healthy and confident in our bodies!" So get out there, America, and start moving! Start feeding your families right, getting in those workouts, and teaching your kids that their health is worth the effort. The healthier we are, the stronger we are-not just physically but mentally and emotionally. A nation that prioritizes the health and well-being of its children is a nation that's truly on the right track.

In the end, it comes down to this: Are we going to keep making excuses, or are we going to make a change? Yes, it's easier to point fingers at the government or societal issues, but we have power within our own homes. We can change what our children eat, how they move, and ultimately how they feel. And if we don't? We're setting them up for a life of frustration, horrible health habits, and severe physical and medical issues as they grow older.

Chapter 27

American Music and Our Children:

It's Time for a Change

At first glance, the topic of music and its impact on children might seem like it's veering off course from the critical issue of school shootings. But, in reality, it's not. Much like my previous discussions on food, nutrition, and the health of our nation's children, this subject provides insight into the subtle yet powerful forces shaping the tone and attitudes of the next generation. Both music and nutrition might seem like minor factors, but they play a significant role in how we mold our youth. These factors, seemingly simple yet profoundly impactful, are areas where we, as Americans, can start making changes to combat the climate of racism, violence, and overall discontent that plagues our society.

Consider this: food and music, two staples of daily life, have the power to influence the mind, body, and soul. When we feed our children and youth a steady diet junk-whether it is processed food or music that glorifies violence and debases human dignity-we are setting them on a path that is anything but healthy. These are not just passive influences; they actively shape how our young people think, feel, and act. And when those influences lean toward the negative, the results can be devastating.

This isn't about pointing fingers or casting judgment on any particular genre of music or anyone's cultural food choices. It's about recognizing the subtle yet pervasive ways in which we, as a society, are contributing to the destruction of our children when we allow the glorification of violence and racism to permeate the music industry or when we ignore the impact of poor nutrition on a child's development, we are, in essence, grooming the next generation to continue these harmful cycles.

Let's be clear: the examples of how bad food and music can destroy the mind, body, and soul of our nation's children and youth are not trivial. They are, in fact, profound indicators of deeper societal issues. These are not just lifestyle choices; they are reflections of the values we are passing down to our children. And suppose those values include a disregard for health, well-being, and respect for others. In that case, it should come as no surprise when we see the results manifest in angry, disillusioned youth who are capable of extreme violence.

Let's not pretend we don't see the connection. We feed our kids sugar-laden snacks on every holiday, pump them full of fast food, pizza, sodas, and candy, and fail to prioritize any form of physical fitness. At the same time, we allow easy access to guns and drugs on the streets while creating music that glamorizes prostitution and gun violence. And then we have the nerve to act surprised when our children grow up angry, lost, and in dire need of mental health support. Really,

America? You're shocked that we have an issue with youth shooting up their schools? I wonder why that could be.

It's not just a matter of bad examples; it's about the environment we've created. An environment where unhealthy food, a lack of fitness, easy access to weapons, and toxic cultural messages all contribute to a crisis of identity and purpose among our youth. We have created a breeding ground for discontent, where the seeds of violence are sown daily, and then we act bewildered when they take root and grow into tragedy.

So, yes, the topic of music and its impact on children is very much relevant to the broader conversation about school shootings. It's all interconnected. The way we feed our children's bodies and minds is directly linked to the outcomes we see in their mental health. And while this might be a study for another day, let's not lose sight of the urgency here. This isn't just a matter of preference or taste; it's a matter of life and death.

If we, as adults, want to indulge in unhealthy food or listen to whatever music we choose, that's our prerogative. But we cannot, in good conscience, impose those same destructive choices on our children. We cannot have children. We cannot continue to stuff them full of sugar, neglect their physical health, allow them easy access to guns, and then expect them to thrive in a society that glorifies violence.

The reality is simple: **Bad Diets and Bad Music Create Bad Kids.**

Unless we take serious action to address these issues, we

are dooming our children to a future filled with anger, violence, and despair. This isn't just a wake-up call; it's a call to action. It's time we start caring about the little things because those little things are what ultimately shape the next generation. If we truly want to ensure a better future for our children and youth, we need to start by changing the way we nourish their bodies and minds today.

So, what's it going to be, America? Will we continue to sit idly by, or will we finally take responsibility for the world we are creating? The choice is ours, and the time to act is now.

Bad Music and the Future of Our Children: Are We Really Surprised?

As a songstress and musician traversing the vibrant landscapes of blues, gospel, rock, punk, funk, and jazz, I have a deep appreciation for how these genres resonate with the very soul and emotions of adults. They are uniquely crafted to capture our experiences, our joys, our pains, and our resilience. Yet, it's not just us, the grown-ups, who are tuning in. America's children and youth are also listening-and therein lies the problem.

The melodies that once inspired change and revolution now seem to peddle an unnerving array of dark and destructive themes. Gone are the days of music purely as a beacon of hope and unity; today's songs often glorify gun violence, racism, and, more alarmingly, all things demonic. It's as if we've handed our children the keys to a musical kingdom where shadows reign supreme, and frankly, it's time to ask: What on earth are we doing?

Let's Talk About the Real Crisis:

Between bad nutrition, contaminated water, lack of sleep, insufficient love and guidance from the adults around them, and poor school systems, our children are facing an uphill battle. Throw in easy access to guns and exposure to music that romanticizes chaos and vice, and it becomes painfully clear: we are in the midst of a crisis that transcends mere artistic expression. It's not just a few bad notes; it's an entire symphony of societal neglect playing out in real-time.

America's youth, caught in this tumult, aren't merely passive listeners-they're absorbing these messages. And despite living in what is often hailed as the greatest nation on earth, they are forced to question where they can find safety and protection. Seriously, America, this shouldn't even be a question! In a country that prides itself on freedom and opportunity, our children should never feel trapped in a corner, fighting against the tide of hypocrisy, hatred, and chaos.

Let's Get Real:

Let's not mince words here. America, you are waging a civil war against your future-your children-and it's high time we face the facts. Yes, kids need protection from school shootings, but they also need shielding from harmful influences that begin at home with poor nutrition, unhealthy lifestyle choices, and, yes, the music that's poisoning their minds. We must adopt laws and policies that don't just address immediate dangers but safeguard their holistic well-being.

We, as adults, bear the responsibility of creating an environment where our children can thrive rather than merely survive. It's time to "Get it together, America!" Let's stop with the excuses and start with solutions. Do we really want our children to become collateral damage in our societal power struggles? Or do we dare to envision a future where our children are protected, nourished, and inspired to build something better?

A Call for Unity and Action:

This is a rallying cry for unity and love, a slightly sarcastic, perhaps, yet passionate plea for action. We must embrace the truth: America is failing its children and youth. But it doesn't have to be this way. We can turn the tide, but only if the adults in the room decide to grow up and change course. It's time to prioritize good nutrition, health and fitness, and positive influences in every aspect of a child's life.

As a fitness professional, I can't help but suggest a radical idea: a national day of fitness in America! Imagine the transformation as children begin to see themselves not as pawns in a chaotic world but as empowered individuals capable of making healthy choices for their futures. What if they could look forward to something brighter and better? Wouldn't that be a legacy worth leaving?

Let's provide our children with a vision of a positive future rather than the chaos that currently defines the world around them. We owe it to them and to ourselves to ensure that the soundtrack of their lives is one of hope, strength, and unity.

So, America, are we ready to make a change? Will we continue to tune out the cries of our children, drawing them out with the cacophony of our own making? The choice is ours, and the stakes couldn’t be higher. Let's choose wisely.

Conclusion

A Call to Action: Ending Madness & A Message of Love: To Black and Brown Children Across America

To the children and youth of America, especially our Black and Brown communities, I want you to know that you are seen, you are valued, and your struggles matter. This book is written with you in mind, and I promise to do everything in my power to push for a future where you have the opportunities, resources and love you deserve. But I cannot do this alone. This fight is bigger than one person-it's a call to the entire nation. It will take all of us-families, communities, policymakers, and every concerned American-to come together and create real change.

Let's be honest: there's a grim possibility looming ahead. My research on 15 Black and Brown families in Los Angeles, San Juan, Puerto Rico, and the Bronx uncovered something alarming. The very environment that's been breeding school shooters among young white males could easily produce the same tragic outcomes among our Black and Brown youth. The reality is both groups share a common experience of living in a society riddled with racism, violence, and neglect. That is truly disturbing. This isn't just my conclusion-leading studies from institutions like California State University San Bernardino's Center for the Study of Hate and Extremism, the FBI, the APA, and the Washington Post all agree. The data points to a heartbreaking truth: the same factors that push white youth into committing these horrific acts could be pushing Black and Brown youth onto the same path. America needs to wake up to this reality.

It's time for our leaders to stop talking in circles and take real action. We need policies that address school shootings head-on while preserving our rights. It's not just about gun control; it's about fostering healthier homes with better nutrition, promoting fitness and well-being, and filling our households with love, understanding, and faith. America, we need to take a hard look at how we're contributing to the destruction of Black and Brown dreams and fix it. Why not start with something as simple as a national day of fitness and wellness for all Americans? Let's make sure our children feel important, valued, and protected, regardless of race or culture. After all, we claim to be "One Nation Under God, Indivisible." So let's live up to that and stand united against the issues threatening our kid's future.

We, as Americans, have the power to do this. We've stood together before, and we can do it again. Together, we can end this school shooting nightmare and give our children what they deserve. I know this conclusion is a bit unconventional, but that's because this issue is anything but typical. To everyone who is stuck with this book, thank you. I hope it left you inspired to fight for change, to stand against school shootings, gun violence, and the systemic racism poisoning our country. Let's commit to making 2024 the year we finally prioritize our children. Let's stop labeling anyone as a "minority." That word carries the weight of racism all by itself. From now on, let's just be "Americans." And remember, it doesn't matter who wins the 2024 Presidential election. What matters is what they plan to do about the serious issues our country faces-like gun violence among our youth. Trump, Obama, Biden, Harris, Dr. Cornel West, or whoever else-we need tangible results. We need a President who leads with integrity and addresses these problems head-on. That's what true leadership looks like: protecting the most vulnerable among us, our children and youth.

This epidemic of violence is an issue that transcends political lines. It is a crisis of humanity, a test of our nation's moral compass. Yet here we are, fighting amongst ourselves while our children watch, learn, and suffer. Are we teaching them that this is the best we can do? Are we, the adults, content to bicker and blame while they bear the consequences of our inaction?

What message are we sending to the next generation? That it's okay for their lives to be at risk every day they step into a classroom? Will the government do nothing to protect them because their lives are worth less than political posturing?

We must demand better. We must demand that our leaders stand up and take action. Reform gun laws, implement measures specifically designed to prevent school shootings, and prioritize the safety and security of our children above all else. Anything less is a disgrace to the nation we claim to love. The time for America to make a change is now!

The blood of our children should not be the cost of freedom. It should not be the price we pay for political gridlock and governmental apathy.

We should be horrified that we are the only nation where school shootings are a regular occurrence. We should be ashamed that we are leaving a legacy of fear and violence for our children to inherit.

America, wake up! This is not the future we want for our children. We must act now, not tomorrow, or next week, or next year, but right now. Every day we delay is another day we risk more innocent lives being lost.

Our children deserve better. They deserve to learn and grow in a world where they are safe, protected, and valued. They deserve to be remembered, not as just victims of a broken system, but as catalysts for change. As long as school shootings continue to plague our nation, we should treat these tragedies as the national emergency they truly are.

This isn't just a call for gun reform; it's a demand for accountability. Our government owes it to us, to the parents, to the children, to the future of this nation, to take decisive action. If they can't or won't protect our children, then they should at least have the decency to honor those we've lost as they would our fallen soldiers.

But even more than that, they should have the courage to enact real change. Because if we don't if we continue to do nothing, then we are complicit in every tragedy that follows. We are guilty of valuing guns over lives, power over safety, and politics over people.

It's about gun control; it's about fostering healthier homes with better nutrition, promoting fitness and well-being, and filling our households with love, understanding, and faith. America, we need to take a hard look at how we're contributing to the destruction of Black and Brown dreams and fix it. Why not start with something as simple as a national day of fitness and wellness for all Americans? Or how about promoting positive music that glorifies life and good health? Let's make sure our children feel important, valued, and protected, regardless of race or culture. After all, we claim to be "One Nation Under God, Indivisible." So let's live up to that and stand united against the issues threatening our kid's future.

I do believe it's time for America to face the music. It's time for us to wake up from this nightmare we've created and do something about it. The blood of our children cries out for justice, action, and change. Are we listening?

Let's not wait until another child becomes a statistic. Let's not wait until another family is shattered. Let's not wait any longer. It's time to end this madness and reclaim the sanctity of our schools as places of learning, not battlegrounds.

America, it's time to stand up and demand change. Our children, our future, are depending on us. Are we going to let them down?

We owe them nothing less than our very best efforts to ensure their safety and to honor those we've already lost by ensuring that no more lives are senselessly sacrificed. America, this is our moment. Let's take that first step together. It could change the entire course of our nation. God Bless America once again. May God continue to Bless the whole world. In Jesus Christ of Nazareth's mighty name, I pray, Amen.

A Message to the World:

To every nation on this beautiful planet, I humbly urge you to take a deep breath, step back from your strategies of force and military might, and reflect on a different kind of battle-one that requires more than armies and weapons. This battle is for the hearts, minds, and souls of your country's most precious resource: your children and youth. It's easy to focus on national defense and external threats, but what about the internal threat residing within our borders-the rising tide of school shootings, gun violence, and the breakdown of young lives before they even have a chance to flourish? Protecting a nation is not just about guarding its borders but nurturing the next generation within those borders with the same intensity and commitment.

Imagine for a moment how truly awesome the world would be if we just knocked it off-yes, knocked off all the hatred, racism, wars, and division. Imagine a world where we prioritize feeding our children healthy meals instead of feeding them hate, where we offer better schools, more opportunities for success, and a deeper sense of community rather than bombarding them with messages of conflict and violence. Every child deserves a chance to grow up in an environment where they are loved, valued, and protected, not just from outside threats but from the dangers lurking in their neighborhoods and homes. Let's be real, world: We are consumed by conflict, drowning in divisions, and somehow, in the madness of it all, we forget that the real power lies in unity, peace, and mutual respect. Yes, I know this might sound like "crazy-hippie-talk" to some, but it's not. It's a vision for a world where we choose love over hate, peace over war, and unity over division.

The song says it best: "And I think to myself, what a wonderful world." But is it really so wonderful? It could be if we just took a moment to change our hearts and minds. I'm not here to argue about your religious beliefs, your political stances, or even your worldview. I'm only concerned with what lies within your heart. If we, as individuals and as nations, could commit to truly seeing one another as valuable, worthy human beings deserving of love, dignity, and peace, then the world could indeed become the wonderful place Louis Armstrong dreamed about in his song. We've done it before- just think back to the global outpouring of unity and solidarity in the wake of George Floyd's tragic death. People of all races, religions, genders, and nationalities came together in outrage and love, demanding justice and change. If we could unite, then surely, we can unite again to protect our children from the scourge of violence and despair that threatens their future.

So, let's take a lesson from that moment and realize that we can achieve something just as powerful, just as beautiful if we decide to act now. We can come together as a world where they feel safe, nurtured, and loved. We've seen glimpses of this potential in our shared history; now it's time to make it a permanent reality. If you're reading this, you were alive when the world stood up for justice before. You witnessed it. Let's make sure we witness it again- this time for the sake of our children's future.

God Bless America.
May God continue to bless the whole world.
Amen.

Special Acknowledgement

Dear Readers with No Religious Affiliations: Your Decision to Pick Up This Book is Truly Admirable

In a world filled with diverse beliefs and backgrounds, it's essential to remember that what truly matters is not your religion- or lack thereof- but the kindness in your heart and the attitude you bring to the world. Whether you're an atheist, a Satan worshiper, a witch, a warlock, or a member of an organized religion, none of these labels define your capacity for love, compassion, and kindness. I've met some of the most incredible, loving, and caring people who have no religious affiliations at all, yet they live their lives with joy and generosity.

The author of this book speaks boldly about God, not only out of personal love for God, Amen, but also because, as Americans, we often proclaim our love for God too. Or did I just imagine that whole "One Nation Under God" thing?

What truly makes the United States so amazing is that your neighbors could be from an entirely different country, speak a language other than English, and hold unfamiliar beliefs- or none at all. Yet, they can be a blast to hang out with, and you might find you have a ton in common despite coming from completely different worlds. That's what makes us so awesome. That's what makes America Great! It's us, the United States citizens. And it's up to all of us, regardless of our beliefs, to come together and love one another despite our differences. Let's show American children and youth how to unite in love and understanding.

The author bases much of this work on the words "One Nation Under God, Indivisible." It's because of those words, the principles we say America stands for, that this work finds its driving force. But we sure aren't acting like a country that loves God as much as we claim to. Why is that America?

To all the readers still with me, I extend my sincere thanks. This book isn't about changing anyone's beliefs. No, it's about seeing that as long as you're an adult living here in "The United States of Freaking Awesome America," you have a role to play in this "American drama," and that role is: Be kind to our nation's children and youth. Be an example in your everyday life to all the young people around you. Don't teach our future generations to hate each other. AND WE MUST CUT OUT THIS RACISM ENOUGH ALREADY! NO ONE IS SUPERIOR TO ANYONE ELSE, okay? SO GET OVER YOURSELVES! Perhaps it's your money and status that make some of you act like you have a "stinky attitude" of supposed superiority. Knock it off, America! This "Old Demon" called "Racism" must die, and we're the only ones who can kill it.

This book is about unity, our nation's children, and how genuinely living as though we are "One Nation Under God" could transform our nation's future trajectory.

Now, if you don't want to hear about unity, love, and us banding together as a nation to make "We the People" responsible for America's future and how simple kindness could change the hateful environment we have today-well, then, don't read this book. Obviously, you're CLEARLY PART OF

THE PROBLEM, so the author would much rather you sit this one out.

For everyone else who wants to "get their love, unity, and non-racism on," well then, climb aboard this spaceship of love, and let's start teaching American children that "Love is a Lovely Thing!" Thanks to those with no religious beliefs who were still curious enough to open this book, even after seeing the mighty name of God in the title. Amen.

Letter to Former President Obama

Dear Former President Obama,

Please allow me to first start by saying, "Thank You!" You will always and forever be my president. I firmly believe that no one is 100% right or 100% wrong. However, some in our society expect you to enter the White House and wave a magic wand to solve not only America's problems but also the many issues facing Black people in this country. I want you to know that many of us applaud your administration.

You led a country built on racism to the best of your ability. On Tuesday, January 20, 2009, at the West Front of the United States Capitol in Washington, D.C., as you were sworn in as the 4th president of the United States, you set the record for attendance for any event held in Washington, D.C. With combined attendance numbers, media coverage, television viewership, and internet traffic, your inauguration was the most observed event by a global audience.

Because of you, little Black boys all over America aspired to be more like you when they grew up rather than imitating their favorite athletes or rappers. I can never thank you enough for the tears of both disbelief and sheer joy that your win brought to the eyes of my grandparents, both in their mid-80s, my parents, and, at the time, my 101-year-old great-great-great-aunt. The moment was palpable and priceless.

As we are now in the midst of the 2024 presidential debate, the racial tension among many Americans is unfortunately at its peak. Between Donald Trump and Kamala Harris, this presidential race is riddled with excitement and intriguing moments. However, I pray that both candidates use this office of the presidency to unify our great nation and not further divide it. (And if not, maybe we can find a way to clone you? Just kidding... sort of.)

You made the best decision of all by marrying Michelle Obama. Her strength and character speak volumes to Black women all over the world, along with the poise, grace, and maturity of your two beautiful, now adult daughters, Sasha and Malia Obama. Your role as the first Black U.S. president has done far more wonders for the mental health, *hearts, and souls of America's children and youth than you could ever imagine.*

Although many have negative things to say about your time in office, I am quite thankful for you and the way you made the office of the presidency look "so fly!" (Seriously, how did you manage to make presidential speeches sound like a mixtape intro?)

In the words of my late grandfather, Mr. Frank Theodore Jones, who served 30 years in the United States Air Force, "No matter what they say about you, you're alright with me, kid!" I could go on for days proclaiming how much you and the first family set such a strong and united Black Family.

Please allow me to close by saying no matter what negative opinions some may have about you, never forget that you have a Father in Heaven who loves you more than you could possibly imagine. He is extremely loving and kind, and there is nothing in life that God can't fix. Thank you for your service as President of the United States of America, and may God continue to bless and watch over your family and our country forever and ever. Amen.

With deepest gratitude and respect,

- L. T. Webb

Letter to Candace Owen

"To Candace Owens: An Ode of Love, Respect, and Understanding"

Dear Candace-

First and foremost, I want to express my deep appreciation for you. As a fellow Black woman, I'm proud of everything you've accomplished and the courage you've shown. Like my Aunt, Brenda always said, "It's not just about what you say but how you say it, and you manage to articulate your thoughts with grace and clarity." While some in the Black community may misunderstand your intentions, there are many of us who hear you loud and clear. So please, keep shouting and making your voice heard.

The racism that exists within the Black community- whether due to social class, skin tone, or other divisive issues-is a reality that you bravely confront. You take the negative, sometimes violent, comments directed at you from outside our community, who wouldn't dare to stand alongside you and fight for any cause, and you handle them like a champ. It's not easy to face disparaging remarks about your "Blackness" from other Black people, yet you rise above it all with unwavering strength.

The support you might always receive from some parts of our community is more than made up for by the countless people worldwide who admire and respect you. And let's not forget, you have the greatest support of all God's love. Keep spreading His message, and continue being the strong, amazing young woman that you are.

I must admit, I wasn't your biggest fan in the beginning. But after taking the time to listen and study your words over the years, I am now- and have been for quite a while- a Candace Owens fan! You have a unique perspective and the bravery to express it, which is something I have grown to admire deeply. In a world that oftentimes challenges the voices of intelligent black women, your resilience is inspiring.

I" 'd like to remind you that even Jesus Christ was treated with disdain and ridicule. Yet, He persisted in His mission. As a Black woman living in the United States, where our voices are often marginalized, I Respect and admire your determination to be heard. The author has the utmost respect for what you aim to accomplish as a Christian, a wife, a mother, an American citizen, and, of course, as a beautiful Black woman. We hear you, Sis!

Many in the Black community love and support

you, myself included. Thank you for your love of God and for addressing the pressing issues in our society today. You are setting a powerful example for young Black girls who may aspire to engage in politics because of your trailblazing efforts. Your work is vital, and it matters.

From one older, educated Black woman to a young, educated Black woman, I want to acknowledge the racial challenges we both face in America. As a fellow lover of Jesus Christ and an advocate for the growth and prosperity of our great nation, I commend you. Thank you for being a voice of reason and for continuing to pave the way for others. Your courage, tenacity, and unwavering faith are truly commendable. God bless you and your growing family. Amen.

With heartfelt appreciation and respect, - The Author

Author's Notes

Getting Rid of the Term "Minority" America's Call to Action: Uniting for the Future of Our Children and Youth

Hey America! I'm no psychologist, but I firmly believe that a crucial step toward dismantling racism in our society could be as simple as vowing to stop referring to Black and Brown citizens as "Minorities." This label, while seemingly neutral, carries a heavy load of historical and societal baggage that perpetuates feelings of inferiority and exclusion. By continuing to use this term, we unwittingly reinforce the very structures of racism and inequality that we claim to oppose.

The word "Minority," when used to describe Black and Brown children and their families in America, is more than just a label-it is a subtle but powerful reminder of the deep-seated racism that still thrives in this country. This term is not just an innocent demographic designation; it is a word loaded with connotations that mark an entire group of people as "less-than," inherently positioning them as inferior to a so-called "Majority." It is high time we confront this issue as a nation and engage in an open conversation about the damaging effects this word has on the lives and self-perceptions of those who are labeled as such. Why is it that in a country founded on principles of freedom and equality, we still hold onto a term that is inherently unequal and demeaning? Perhaps it's time for America to take a vote-literally. If put to a democratic vote in each state, I am confident that the overwhelming majority of Americans would support getting rid of this harmful label. The word "Minority" needs to be retired, not just from our vocabulary but from our collective mindset.

The author's passion for this subject burns brightly because this label has profound psychological and social consequences. Being branded a "Minority" from birth not only affects Black and Brown children's sense of identity but also reinforces the systemic barriers that keep them marginalized. This term is a constant reminder that, in the eyes of society, they are viewed as "less-than" and that feelings of inferiority can follow them throughout their lives, shaping their opportunities, self-worth, and even their interactions with others. The subtle but persistent messaging that comes with this word- this constant reminder of one's supposed inferior status- is both damaging and infuriating. If this term is not based solely on population statistics, then what is it really rooted in? Who, then, are the so-called "Majority"? Why is it that this group typically consists of people with less melanin in their skin? Are they claiming superiority due to socioeconomic factors, or is this just another manifestation of American racism dressed up as a demographic term?

To dig deeper, we must question the motives behind this label. Let's not kid ourselves: much of what the so-called "Majority" claims as their own- whether in wealth, power, or privilege- was built off the backs of Black slaves and sustained by the labor of Latin and Mexican populations. The notion that any group is inherently superior is as outdated as it is offensive. We are all human, all fallible, and in the eyes of God, we are all equal. Scripture reminds us that we are but "dirty rags" in need of grace. Yet, rather than offering grace to others, many still cling to racism, allowing it to dictate their view of themselves and others. This needs to change.

Maybe in the future, the author will explore this issue in depth in a book solely dedicated to the term "Minority" and the countless ways it continues to harm Black and Brown communities in America. For now, this introduction serves as a call to action for Americans to stop and think about the words we use and the subtle yet powerful ways they shape our society. Words matter. By the way, growing up, I would always hear the phrase, "Sticks and stones may break my bones, but words will never hurt me." The author of this phrase is quite sadly mistaken and is in desperate need of a few one-hour-long sessions with a skilled psychiatrist. Words hurt, and they hurt badly. I am of the belief that, oftentimes, people may not remember exactly what you said verbatim; however, they will always remember how what you said made them feel." Words matter. Labels matter. And if America is serious about healing racial divides, it's time to get rid of this harmful and derogatory label. Let's start by retiring the word "Minority," and maybe, just maybe, we can begin to pave the way for a more just and equal society where no one is made to feel inferior from the day they are born. After all, we are all God's children, and none of us is superior to one another.

Imagine the transformative impact if we collectively decided to retire the term "Minority" from our lexicon. This change alone could serve as a powerful catalyst for profound social transformation. It would signify a rejection of the idea that any group of people is inherently less important or less valuable than another. By removing this label, we take a significant step toward reshaping societal perceptions and fostering a sense of equality and respect. It's not just about the words we use; it's about changing the narrative that has long positioned Black and Brown individuals as peripheral or subordinate.

Think about it: how often do we overlook subtle ways in which language perpetuates discrimination? The term "Minority" implies a status of lesser importance, subtly suggesting that those it describes are secondary in value and significance. By eliminating this term, we can start to break down these damaging connotations and promote a more inclusive and equitable society. This shift would not only alter how individuals see themselves but also how they are seen by others. It's about much more than semantics; it's about changing the way we think and act.

Furthermore, taking this step could set a precedent for addressing other forms of discrimination and exclusion. It represents a willingness to confront uncomfortable truths and make meaningful changes. This could inspire further efforts to eradicate other derogatory terms and practices of inequality. In essence, erasing the label "Minority" could be the first domino to fall into a broader movement toward genuine equality and social justice.

In conclusion, while I'm not an expert, it seems clear that eliminating the term "Minority" could play a pivotal role in advancing racial equality in the United States. It's a simple yet profound change that could lead to a significant shift in how we view and treat each other. Let's begin this journey toward a more just society by reconsidering the language we use and striving for a future where every individual is valued equally, free from the constraints of outdated and harmful labels.

God & Love

"Be completely humble and gentle; be patient, bearing with **one another** in **love**."

— Ephesians 4:2

"Above all, **love each other** deeply because **love** covers over a multitude of sins."

— 1 Peter 4:8

4 Love is patient, **love** is kind. It does not envy, it does not boast, it is not proud. **5** It does not dishonor others; it is not self-seeking; it is not easily angered, and it keeps no record of wrongs. **6 Love** does not delight in evil but rejoices with the truth. 7It always protects, always trusts, always hopes, always perseveres. **8 Love** never fails. But where there are prophecies, they will cease; where there are tongues, they will be stilled; where there is knowledge, it will pass away.

— 1 Corinthians 13: 4-8

"Let no debt remain outstanding, except the continuing debt to **love one another**, for whoever **loves others** has fulfilled the law."

— Romans 13:8

"A new command I give you: **Love one another** as I have **loved** you, so you must **love one another**."

— John 13:34

"For God so **loved the world** that He gave His one and only Son, that whosoever believes in Him shall not perish but have eternal life."

— John 3:16

"But God demonstrates his **love for us** in this: While we were still sinners, Christ died for us."

— Romans 5:8

7 Dear friends, let us love one another, for **love** comes from God. Everyone who **loves** has been born of God and knows God. Whoever does not love does not know God because **God is love**.

— 1 John 4:7-8

"And now these three remain: faith, hope, and love. But the greatest of these is love."

— 1 Corinthians 13:13

"And over all these virtues put on **love,** which binds them **all together** in perfect unity."

— Colossians 3:14

"Hatred stirs up conflict, but love covers all wrongs."

— Proverbs 10:12

God's Words to the Leaders of Nations

"As leaders, you are responsible for those you lead. These people are looking to you for guidance, like little children. We have a responsibility to lead and to lead well."

— Matthew 18:6

"Her officials within her are like wolves tearing their prey; they shed blood and kill people to make unjust gain."

— Ezekiel 22:27

"You have despised my holy things and desecrated my Sabbaths."

— Ezekiel 22:8

"Your rulers are rebels, partners with thieves; they all love bribes and chase after gifts. They do not defend the cause of the fatherless; the widow's case does not come before them."

— Isaiah 1:23

"Woe to those who make unjust laws, to those who issue oppressive decrees."

— Isaiah 10:1

"If a ruler listens to lies, all his officials become wicked."

— Proverbs 29:12

"Woe to the shepherds who are destroying and scattering the sheep of my pasture!" declares the Lord. Therefore, this is what the Lord, the God of Israel, says to the shepherds who tend my people: "Because you have scattered my flock and driven them away and have not bestowed care on them, I will bestow punishment on you for the evil you have done," declares the Lord.

— Jeremiah 23:1-2

"Like a roaring lion or a charging bear is a wicked ruler over a helpless people."

— Proverbs 28:15

"Israel's watchmen are blind; they all lack knowledge; they are all mute dogs; they cannot bark; they lie around and dream; they love to sleep. They are dogs with mighty appetites; they never have enough. They are shepherds who lack understanding; they all turn their own way, and they seek their own gain. "Come," each one cries, "let me get wine! Let us drink our fill of beer! And tomorrow will be like today, or even far better."

— Isaiah 56: 10-12

"For rebellion is like the sin of divination, and arrogance like the evil of idolatry. Because you have rejected the word of the Lord, he has rejected you as king."

— 1 Samuel 15:23

"He changes times and seasons; he removes kings and sets up kings; he gives wisdom to the wise and knowledge to those who have understanding."

— Daniel 2:21

"First of all, then, I urge that supplications, prayers, intercessions, and thanksgiving be made for all people, for kings and all who are in high positions, that we may lead a peaceful and quiet life, godly and dignified in every way."

— 1 Timothy 2: 1-2

"For what shall it profit a man if he shall gain the whole world and lose his soul?"

— Mark 8:36

"Not only does God speak these words to the leaders of nations, but God also gives instructions to the population about how they should pray for the leaders of nations. The Bible urges us to turn to prayer for all things. According to the book of Ephesians, God's desire is for us to pray "on all occasions with all kinds of prayers and requests."

— Ephesians 6:18

As a nation, we are encouraged to pray for our Presidents, Senators, Governors, and our state legislatures. Our prayer should be that God provides each of them with wisdom and strength and that they allow God to guide their decisions.

The goal we should have in our hearts and our minds is that all of us need to keep our nation and its leaders in prayer at all times. As you go to prayer, please consider our nations leaders, whether they are good or bad. Pray that God will continue to intercede if that is what's needed, or pray that God will provide our nation's leaders with peace and a sound mind as they move forth with their decision-making process and also for sound rest as they labor.

> "Yet give attention to your servant's prayer and his plea for mercy, Lord my God. Hear the cry and the prayer that your servant is praying in your presence this day." **1 Kings 8:28**

> "From one man he made all the nations, that they should inhabit the whole earth; and he marked out their appointed times in history and the boundaries of their lands." **Acts 17:26**

> "He will judge between the nations and will settle disputes for many peoples. They will beat their swords into plow-shares and their spears into pruning hooks. Nation will not take up sword against nation, nor will they train for war anymore." **Isaiah 2:4**

> "All the ends of the earth will remember and turn to the Lord, and all the families of the nations will bow down before him, for dominion belongs to the Lord, and he rules over the nations." **Psalms 22: 27-28**

“Let everyone be subject to the governing authorities, for there is no authority except that which God has established. The authorities that exist have been established by God.” **Romans 13:1**

“Also, seek the peace and prosperity of the city to which I have carried you into exile. Pray to the Lord for it because if it prospers, you too will prosper.” **Jeremiah 29:7**

“The nations will fear the name of the Lord; all the kings of the earth will revere your glory.” **Psalm 102:15**

“The fear of the Lord is the beginning of wisdom, and knowledge of the Holy One is understanding.” **Proverbs 9:10**

“Why do the nations conspire and the peoples plot in vain? The kings of the earth rise up, and the rulers band together against the Lord and against the anointed, saying, 'Let us break their chains and throw off their shackles.' The One enthroned in heaven laughs; the Lord scoffs at them. He rebukes them in his anger and terrifies them in his wrath, saying, “I have installed my king on Zion, my holy mountain.” I will proclaim the decree: He said to me, “You are my son; today, I have become your father as I and I will make the nations your inheritance, the ends of your possession. You will break them with a rod of iron; you will crush them to pieces like pottery.” Therefore, you kings, be wise; be warned, you rulers of the earth. Serve the Lord with fear and celebrate his rule with trembling. Kiss his son, or he will be angry, and your way will lead to your destruction, for his wrath can flare up in a moment. Blessed are all who take refuge in all the nations will be gathered before him, and he will separate the people one from another as a shepherd separates the sheep from the goats. He will put the sheep on his right and the goats on his left. "Then the King will say to those on his right, "Come, you who are blessed by my Father; take your inheritance, the kingdom prepared for you since the creation of the world." **Matthew 25: 32-34**

"For the Lord Most High is awesome, the great King over all the earth. He subdued nations under us, peoples under our feet. He chose our inheritance for us, the pride of Jacob, whom he loved. God has ascended amid shouts of joy, the Lord amid the sounding of trumpets. Sing praises to God, sing praises; sing praises to our King. Sing praises. For God is the King of all the earth; sing to him a psalm of praise. God reigns over the nations; God is seated on his holy throne. The nobles of the nations assemble as the people of the God of Abraham, for the kings of the earth belong to God; he is greatly exalted." **Psalm 47: 2-9**

"In your relationships with one another, have the same mindset as Christ Jesus: Who, being in very nature God, did not consider equality with God something to be used to his own advantage; rather, he made himself nothing by taking the very nature of a servant, being made in human likeness. And being found in appearance as a man, he humbled himself by becoming obedient to death-even death on a cross! Therefore God exalted him to the highest place and gave him the name that is above every name, that at the name of JESUS, every knee should bow, in heaven and on earth and under the earth, and every tongue acknowledge that JESUS CHRIST is LORD, to the glory of GOD the FATHER." **Philippians 2: 5-11**

"A nation that prays together. Stays together."

- The Author

Work Cited

1. The Holy Bible: King James Version (KJV). Harper Collins, 2001.
2. The New Revised Standard Version (NRSV) Bible. Oxford University Press, 1989.
3. The New International Version (NIV) Bible. Zondervan, 2011.
4. Webb, L.T.. "How Gun Violence and School Shootings in America Affect Black and Brown Children and Youth." Ethnographic Study- Los Angeles, Puerto Rico, and New York (2019 - 2023).
5. Webb, L. T. "How Racism, Violence, Terrorism and Socioeconomic Disparities in Black and Brown Communities Affect Children and Youth." Ethnographic Study- Los Angeles (2019-2020), Puerto Rico (2020-2023), New York (2021).
6. Steve Harvey, "Prayer Changes Things," May 23, 2019.
7. "NewYork Times: Dylan Roof Found Guilty in Charleston Church Massacre" by Alan Blinder and Keven Sack, December 15, 2016; "GQ: A Most American Terrorist: The Making of Dylan Roof" By Rachel Kaadzi Ghansah, August 21, 2017.
8. Kendi, Ibram X. *"How to Be an Antiracist." One World, 2019.
9. Grisham, Kevin. "The Globalization of Terrorism: Political Science Perspectives." Palgrave Macmillan, 2016.
10. Levin, Brian. "The Psychology of Hate Crimes as Domestic Terrorism." Routledge, 2017.
11. Muhammad, Muhammad R. "Black Youth and Terrorism: Navigating a Hostile Society." New York University Press, 2020.
12. Parsons, Deborah. "Policing and Social Justice: A Critical Approach." Routledge, 2019.
13. Johnson, Umar. "Psycho-Academic Holocaust: The Special Education and ADHD Wars Against Black Boys." Prince of Pan-Afrikanism Publishing, 2013.
14. Johnson, Umar. "The Black Student's Guide to Success: Mastering the Classroom and Beyond." New Afrikan Press, 2019.
15. Kimmel, Michael S. "Angry White Men: American Masculinity at the End of an Era." *Nation Books,*2013, pp. 18-28.

16. Berman, Mark. “The Rising Threat of Domestic Terrorism in America.” The Washington Post, 22 Aug. 2022, www.washingtonpost.com/national/domestic-terrorism-threat/2022/08/22.
17. Parker, Ashley, and Matt Zapotosky. "Bidens Push to Combat Domestic Terrorism Comes amid Rising Threats from Extremists.” The Washington Post, 15 June 2021, www.washingtonpost.com/politics/domestic-terrorism-plsn/2021/06/15.
18. Zakrzewski, Cat. “How Social Media Platforms Are Handling Domestic Terrorism Content.” The Washington Post, 10 Oct. 2021, www.washingtonpost.com/technology/2021/10/10 social-media-domestic-terrorism/.
19. Centers for Disease Control and Prevention. “The Public Health Approach to Violence Prevention.” CDC, 13 May 2022, www.cdc.gov/violenceprevention/about/publichealthapproach.html.
20. American Psychological Association. “Understanding Domestic Terrorism: A Psychological Perspective.” APA, 2021, www.apa.org/monitor/2021/10/domestic-terrorism.
21. Garcia, Marisol E., et al. “Community-Based Approaches to Reducing Gun Violence in Los Angeles: A Riverside Perspective.” Journal of Community Health, University of California Riverside, vol. 42, no. 1, 2022, pp. 112-130.
22. “Trump: *Good People on Both Sides."*2017. https://youtu.be/Maq3vu1HYNc?si=MhpKOCrkla0af3LU
23. Steveson, Brenda J., et al. “Reducing Gun Violence Among Youth in Los Angeles: The Role of Education and Community Programs.” Journal of Education for Students Placed at Risk (JESPAR), vol. 24, no. 2, 2019, pp. 130-146.
24. *Rodriguez-Diaz, Carlos E., and Jorge F. Rivas. “Gun Violence Prevention in Puerto Rico: Policies, Challenges, and Community Efforts.” Puerto Rican Journal of Public Health, vol. 45, no. 2, 2019, pp. 27-39.https://doi.org/10.1016/j.pupr.2019.01.005.*
25. Velez, Maria. “The Bronx and the Violence Within: A Study on Gun Violence Among Youth.” *Bronx Review of Social Issues,* vol. 10, no. 2, 2021, pp. 45-67. https://doi.org/10.1007/s10560-021-00768-y.
26. California State University, Los Angeles. (2022). “Evaluation of the Gang Reduction and Youth Development (GRYD) Program.”

27. FBI Uniform Crime Reports. (2023). "Youth Gun Violence Statistics in U.S. Territories."
28. Federal Bureau of Investigation. "2019-2023 Youth Involvement in Domestic Terrorism." FBI.gov.
29. U.S. Department of Education. "Annual Report on School Safety and Discipline." Ed.gov
30. U.S. Department of Justice. "Historical Overview of Major School Shootings in the United States." Justice.gov.
31. National Center for Education Statistics (NCES). "School Crime and Safety." NCES.ed.gov.
32. Los Angeles Police Department (LAPD). "Annual Crime Reports." LAPDOnline.org.
33. Puerto Rico Police Department. "Annual Report." PRPB.gov.
34. New York Police Department (NYPD). CompStat.NYC.gov.
35. Centers for Disease Control and Prevention (CDC). "Nutrition, Physical Activity, and Obesity: Data, Trends, and Maps." CDC.gov.
36. https://youtu.be/r2bwPV-I1vU. December 4, 2014. BBC Hardtalk: Dr. Cornel West talks about the current racial tensions in the U.S. and Obama's reaction.
37. https://youtu.be/CnTPBK4BrNQ. May 22, 2019. Fox News: Are Trump's economic policies helping African Americans?
38. https://youtu.be/qqzo6UYSbRM. June 22, 2015. CNN: Dr. Cornel West reacts to Obama's usage of the N-word.
39. https://youtu.be/2WD27cwfh0o. July 6, 2017. Fox Business: The ongoing effort to curb terrorism.
40. https://youtu.be/yiER4rUrGN8. August 6, 2019. The Daily Show; "What Causes Mass Shootings"

Protecting Discourse On School Shootings and Solutions:

A Fair Use Perspective

T***he Fair Use Act***, as defined under 17 U.S.C. S107, allows for the limited use of copyrighted material without obtaining explicit permission from the rights holders. This protection is particularly important in the context of criticism, comment, news reporting, teaching, scholarship, or research. The content in this book, which addresses the alarming rise in school shootings, the potential future of Black and Brown children mirroring these violent behaviors, and the exploration of solutions through nutrition, health, fitness, and political discourse, falls squarely within the Fair Use doctrine. This work aims to inform, educate, and contribute to the public dialogue on critical issues affecting the United States, particularly in the fields of sociology, social sciences, psychology, theology, and the Second Amendment.

The author's professional background, personal experiences as a former educator and single Black mother, and expertise in conducting ethnographic studies lend credibility to the discussion and conclusions drawn within this book. While the author's insights are informed by a deep understanding of various academic fields, they are ultimately offered as part of a broader scholarly discourse intended to advance understanding and foster meaningful conversation on pressing societal issues. The use of external data, expert opinions, and references to other studies are all conducted in accordance with the Fair Use doctrine, ensuring that the work remains a protected and vital part of the ongoing discussion about school shootings and their impact on American society.

www.ingramcontent.com/pod-product-compliance
Lightning Source LLC
LaVergne TN
LVHW010543160826
845677LV00013B/2981

* 9 7 9 8 8 9 6 9 1 1 0 6 7 *